PARALLEL SOURCE PROBLEMS
IN MEDIEVAL HISTORY

BY

FREDERIC DUNCALF, PH.D.
ADJUNCT PROFESSOR, UNIVERSITY OF TEXAS

AND

AUGUST C. KREY, M.A.
INSTRUCTOR, UNIVERSITY OF ILLINOIS

WITH AN INTRODUCTION BY
PROF. DANA CARLETON MUNRO
OF THE UNIVERSITY OF WISCONSIN

Wipf & Stock
PUBLISHERS
Eugene, Oregon

Wipf and Stock Publishers
199 W 8th Ave, Suite 3
Eugene, OR 97401

Parallel Source Problems in Medieval History
By Duncalf, Frederic and Krey, August C.
ISBN 13: 978-1-55635-198-3
ISBN 10: 1-55635-198-4
Publication date 1/22/2007
Previously published by Harper & Brothers, 1912

CONTENTS

	PAGE
PREFACE	vii
INTRODUCTION	xi

I. THE CORONATION OF CHARLES THE GREAT

- I. The Historical Setting of the Problem 3
- II. The Authors of the Accounts 7
- III. Questions for Study 12
- IV. The Sources 13
    1. The *Annales Laurissenses* 13
    2. The *Annales Laurishamenses* 16
    3. Einhard 18
    4. Theophanis 18
    5. *Life of Leo III.* 19
    6. The Monk of St. Gall 23

II. CANOSSA: FROM OPPENHEIM TO FORESHEIM

- I. The Historical Setting of the Problem 29
- II. The Authors of the Accounts 33
- III. Questions for Study 38
- IV. The Sources 40
    1. The *Annals of Augsburg* 40
    2. The *Agreement at Oppenheim* 41
    3. Lambert of Hersfeld 42

Contents

	PAGE
4. Berthold of Reichenau	56
5. Bernold of St. Blais	72
6. Arnulf	74
7. Bruno's Saxon War	75
8. Anonymous *Life of Henry IV.*	81
9. Bonizo, *The Book to a Friend*	84
10. Donizo	85
11. Letter of Gregory VII. to the German Princes, and Oath of Henry	87

III. THE CAPTURE OF JERUSALEM IN 1099

I. The Historical Setting of the Problem	95
II. The Authors of the Accounts	98
III. Questions for Study	101
IV. The Sources	103
1. The Anonymous *Deeds of the Franks*	103
2. Fulk of Chartres	109
3. Raymond of Agiles	115

IV. THE DEPARTURE OF THE UNIVERSITY FROM PARIS. 1229–1231

I. The Historical Setting of the Problem	137
II. The Authors of the Accounts	141
III. Questions for Study	143
IV. The Sources	145
1. Mathew of Paris	145
2. William of Nangis	148
3. Alberic of Tres Fontes	149
4. Ralph of Coggeshall	150
5. The *Annales of Dunstable*	150
6. Albert of Stade	150

Contents

		PAGE
7. *Chronicle of Fécamp*		151
8. The *Mare Historiarum*		151
9. Order of the Provisors. March 27, 1229		151
10. Letter of Henry III. of England to Masters and Students. July 16, 1229		152
11. Confirmation of Privilege of Philip Augustus. August, 1229		153
12. Letter of Gregory IX. to Bishop of Paris. November 23, 1229		158
13. Letter of Gregory IX. to bishops of Le Mans and Senlis and Archdeacon of Chalons. November 24, 1229		161
14. Letter of Gregory IX. to the King and Queen of France. November 26, 1229		162
15. Letter of Gregory IX. to the Masters and Students. May 10, 1230		164
16. Letter of Gregory IX. to the Masters and Students. February 27, 1231		165
17. Letter of Gregory IX. to the Abbot of St. Germain. April 13, 1231		172
18. Letter of Gregory IX. to the King of France. April 18, 1231		173

V. THE CORONATION OF COLA DI RIENZO

I. The Historical Setting of the Problem 177
II. The Authors of the Accounts 183
III. Questions for Study 187
IV. The Sources 189
   1. Titles used by Cola di Rienzo 189
   2. Letter of Clement VI. to Raymond and Rienzo. June 27, 1347 190

Contents

	PAGE
3. Letter of Rienzo to the Commune of Florence. July 9, 1347	192
4. Letter of Rienzo to a Friend at Avignon. July 15, 1347	193
5. Anonymous *Life of Rienzo*. 1347	196
6. Citation of German Emperor and Electors. August 1, 1347	203
7. Letter of Rienzo to Clement VI. August 5, 1347	207
8. Giovanni Villani: *Historia Universalis*. 1347–8	211
9. Program of the Coronation. August 15, 1347	214
10. Letter of Clement VI. to the Papal Legate. August 21, 1347	216
11. Letter of Rienzo to Clement VI. August 15–31, 1347	217
12. Letter of Rienzo to Rinaldo Orsini. September 17, 1347	220
13. Letter of Rienzo to the Commune of Florence. September 19, 1347	222
14. Letter of Rienzo to Clement VI. October 11, 1347	226
15. Letter of Clement VI. to the Papal Legate. October 12, 1347	231
16. Letter of Clement VI. to People of Rome. December 3, 1347	235
APPENDIX	239
INDEX	245

PREFACE

THE foremost purpose of the present book is to provide parallel source translations, so arranged and equipped with descriptive information that effective training can be given in the use of source material. Although the five problems here presented are based on very definite events in Medieval history, they have also a certain illustrative value. The more intensive study of sources, which the arrangement of the book demands, should arouse greater interest on the part of the average student, and should produce a real appreciation of the nature and importance of sources, as well as a deeper insight into the life and character of the people described.

Enough time must be devoted to each problem to give ample opportunity for careful and thorough study. The class should first be asked to read the entire problem for discussion in recitation. The suggested questions, or others of similar kind, can then be assigned to individual students for written exercises. The student should then be required to search the extracts for every point bearing on his topic, to interprete according to his best judgment,

Preface

and to apply such information as is given in the introductory statements concerning the reliability of the authors and the value of the different selections. While each report should be exhaustive, it should also be concise and definite, and should be carefully criticized and corrected by the instructor.

By thus working on a definite task it is believed that the student will obtain elementary training in the fundamentals of historical method. At the same time the intensive knowledge of certain phases of Medieval history gained thereby will probably be of greater value than would the more extensive information that might be derived from the study of more numerous and varied extracts. The problems are intended to show certain important forces and institutions in their true setting. To a limited extent they possess some degree of continuity. For example, the empire and papacy appear in the documents at different stages of their development. There is abundant opportunity for the student to use much of the information previously obtained from lectures and reading, and the work on the problems can be made a stimulating and practical test of the progress of the class. It is sincerely hoped that the book will enable teachers to obtain better results in the use of source material. Not every teacher has the facilities or the time to explain the background of isolated documents so that the students can understand their importance. These par-

Preface

allel extracts supplement each other and supply enough information to start the student to work on his own initiative. The teacher's time can thus be spent in criticism and suggestion.

We wish to express our grateful indebtedness to Prof. D. C. Munro, from the inspiration of whose teaching the idea in this book has developed. Any merit that the plan may have is largely the fruit of his suggestion and encouragement. Teachers who know the spirit of the history department of the University of Wisconsin will appreciate the importance of the work that it is doing for the improvement of history teaching. We have profited from the work of all who have endeavored to show the possibilities of source study in history teaching. In particular, however, we owe much to some of the *Pennsylvania Translations and Reprints*, to the plan of which the arrangement of this volume is very similar.

F. D.
A. C. K.

INTRODUCTION

IN teaching history the advantages to be gained from the use of some source material are generally recognized. "Experience has proved, not only that the interest of students can be more readily obtained through the vividness of a direct and first-hand presentation, and that knowledge thus gained is more tangible and exact; but that the critical judgment is developed in no slight degree, and the ability as well as the interest for further study thus secured."

The realization of these advantages has led to the preparation and publications of numerous volumes of source books, readings, etc. Unfortunately, the practice has usually been to supply "a multitude of fragments," spread out thinly over the whole chronological period and many classes of topics, with little or no guidance for the students. It is very doubtful whether "the critical judgment" can be developed by the study of a series of disconnected extracts, no matter "how carefully and thoughtfully made." Furthermore, the training to be derived from the use of sources cannot be obtained without

Introduction

intensive work on the part of both teachers and students. A short passage from some source may enliven the narrative and arouse interest, but certainly will not exercise the judgment unless some data are furnished concerning the passage upon which a judgment may be based. In fact, the use of the sources for teaching history has been going through much the same course as the use of the sources for writing history before the critical advance of the nineteenth century. It has been said by Ranke's admirers that before his constructive work the sources were read but not studied. While this statement is not entirely true, it does describe the general usage, and it might be applied, with important reservations, to the so-called source method of teaching in the last generation.

This volume has grown out of the experience of two of my former students. As teachers, both in secondary schools and colleges, they have come to realize the need of a book which would furnish suitable material (and the necessary guidance) for critical and intensive work. They have wisely chosen topics which will interest the students and can be handled either in a high school or college. For each problem they have given important "parallel" accounts, not disconnected fragments. The apparatus which accompanies the sources is amply sufficient for the guidance of either teachers or students, and makes it possible to use this work in

Introduction

private study or in correspondence courses. The topics are well distributed both chronologically and as to subject matter. It will be far better for the teachers to set aside occasionally a definite period of time for intensive work on one of these problems than to attempt each day to do a little with the sources. The pupils will form a much more correct idea of the material from which history is written and the way in which it must be studied. They will also be led to estimate more correctly the value of the different classes of sources. Both teachers and students are to be congratulated on the appearance of this new source book.

DANA CARLETON MUNRO.

University of Wisconsin, October, 1912.

PROBLEM I

I.—The Coronation of Charles the Great

PARALLEL SOURCE PROBLEMS IN MEDIEVAL HISTORY

The Coronation of Charles the Great

I. THE HISTORICAL SETTING OF THE PROBLEM

THE importance of the coronation of Charles the Great depends largely upon what contemporaries and succeeding generations thought of this event. From the disappearance of the Roman Empire down through the Middle Ages the idea persisted that universal empire was the ideal form of state. Men were still unable to free themselves from the political conceptions that they had inherited from Rome, and were mentally incapable of seeing that the old idea, changed as it was in being handed down through the centuries, no longer suited the new conditions that were developing about them. The medieval empire was a false political conception, which was arbitrarily imposed upon society, and which was supported by a public opinion that derived its strength from tradition.

Society in 800 had lost all the essential elements of unity. The invasions had destroyed the old order, and the barbarians had settled in the empire in such numbers that a return to anything like former conditions was

Parallel Source Problems in Medieval History

impossible. Society had disintegrated into small, self-sufficient communities, entirely dependent on agriculture, and with slight need for relations with each other. The demand for commerce had almost ceased, and communication was becoming increasingly difficult. With such conditions existing there was no possibility of recreating the bonds that had given the Roman Empire its unity. Notwithstanding all this, the Frankish race by a remarkable series of conquests had succeeded in welding western Europe into a crude empire. It was held together by force and the personality of Charles. Beneath the surface, forces were at work which were soon to disrupt the Frankish state, but during the reign of Charles men did not realize the weakness of this new political structure. The glorious achievements of the Frankish kings and the intellectual revival, with its admiration for classical literature, produced a confident spirit that enabled men to see in the empire of Charles a likeness to the Roman Empire. Thus the imperial title was given to Charles and the Frankish state became the successor of the empire of Rome.

To understand how this was possible it is necessary to trace the persistence of the Roman tradition, and to understand how the conceptions of what the old empire had been had undergone a decided change. So deeply had Rome impressed itself on the ancient world that it was commonly believed that the empire was eternal. When the Roman government had disappeared, and had been replaced by barbarian kingdoms, men still cherished the delusion that the unity of the empire had not been destroyed, but that the western provinces were still nominally under the rule of the emperor at Constantinople. The armies of Justinian were welcomed in the West, and writers long continued to reckon time by the

The Coronation of Charles the Great

reigns of the eastern emperors. Even the barbarians never entirely lost their respect for Rome. They, too, seemed to believe in its eternity even when it had crumbled beneath their attack. They continued to serve as allies, their kings were flattered by the title of consul or patrician, and the effigy of the emperor continued to adorn their coins. They seemed to prefer to rule as representatives of the emperors rather than by right of conquest. Both conqueror and conquered strove to keep alive the fiction that the unity of the empire was still intact.

However, the conceptions of empire underwent a transformation. The Church taught that the great mission of the Roman Empire was to preserve the Christian religion. As the idea of a universal Church grew up it identified itself with that of universal empire. The names of the Christian emperors were those which were cherished. Thus, the belief in the unity of the empire came to have a religious rather than a political basis. The city of Rome regained something of its former prestige, not as a political capital, but as a religious center. Pilgrims in great numbers journeyed to the eternal city to visit the shrines of the saints. The papacy profited by this, but popes, as well as kings and all of the West, continued to look toward Constantinople with respect, and the vague hope for the political and religious unity of East and West continued.

However, this dream of imperial unity did not prevent the gradual alienation of the West from the East. Friendly relations between popes and emperors were interrupted by controversies about differences in doctrine. The eastern emperors failed to measure up to the new imperial conception of the West. Moreover, the bitter discontent of the provincials with their Arian rulers led them to look to the more immediate aid that they might expect from the Franks, whose orthodoxy greatly aided them in their conquests. The Carolingians were more and more recognized as the defenders of the Christian religion, and worked hand in hand with the Church in converting the peoples whom they conquered. Thus the West was able to see in the Frankish state the Christian state that conformed to its ideas of what an empire should be.

Although Charles received his imperial title from the pope, the attitude of the papacy is not easy to understand. It would seem that Hadrian I., at least, was not anxious to have a new master that he could not control. The papacy had been forced to call in Pepin and his son to check the encroachments of the Lombards, but it was careful to make its own position secure by the donations that it obtained from both Pepin and Charles. Far from encouraging imperial ambitions in the Frankish kings, Hadrian judiciously indicated that the title of patrician was purely honorary. The same pope apparently tried to balance the Byzantine ruler against the Frankish king to his own advantage, and showed no indications of desiring to make Charles an emperor. Events were to precipitate the coronation of 800.

During the last years of the eighth century a changed attitude toward the Byzantine emperors developed. The rule of a woman, Irene, was regarded as wrong, and was interpreted to mean that the throne was really vacant. A proposed marriage between the daughter of Charles and the son of Irene was broken off by the empress. The *Libri Caroli*, which were composed at the court of Charles, were filled with violent criticism of the acts and pretensions of the Byzantine emperors, and were evidently intended to create a public opinion hostile to the eastern empire.

In 795 Hadrian died and was succeeded by Leo III.,

The Coronation of Charles the Great

who was of humble origin, and to whom the Roman nobles, who had supported his aristocratic predecessor, were hostile. Insecure in his position at Rome, Leo was forced to look to Charles for protection. On April 25, 799, the enemies of Leo attacked him and attempted to cut out his tongue and put out his eyes. The pope was rescued, and as soon as he had sufficiently recovered from his injuries he set out for Germany to ask Charles for aid. He found the Frankish king at his camp at Paderborn, and was received with respect and consideration. The enemies of the pope had also forwarded their accusations to the king, upon whom devolved the task of settling the trouble in the Roman Church, if he chose to accept such responsibility. The next year he made the journey to Rome which resulted in his coronation.

II. THE AUTHORS OF THE ACCOUNTS

In studying any historical problem it is first necessary to know when, where, by whom, and how the different accounts were written. The account of an eye-witness, written shortly after the occurrence of the events described, is more reliable than an account composed a generation or more later. Next to the time element the character of the author must be considered. What were his qualifications for accurate observation? Did he have a conscious or unconscious bias that caused him to write a prejudiced narrative? The prejudice of an author may be purely personal, or it may be explained by the circumstances amid which he lived and wrote. The modern historian strives to reach accurate and impartial conclusions by a thorough study of the sources. During the Middle Ages the general mental limitations of the period prevented all writers from reaching such an impartial and impersonal viewpoint. Thus the medieval writer was not only lacking in critical ability, but his account was always colored by the political, religious, and intellectual ideas of the age.

The sources of Carolingian history were written by the educated churchmen. Judged by modern requirements, they were men of very slight knowledge and limited intelligence. Their purpose in writing history was to instruct their readers in the religious significance of historical events. After the coronation of 800 they further endeavored to show that the Roman Empire was restored by the Franks, and that the medieval empire was a direct continuation of the imperial power of the Roman emperors.

Much of the historical writing of the period was in the form of annals, which are brief accounts of events, year by year. This method of writing history has an interesting origin. Many of the feast days of the Church depended upon the day upon which Easter came each year. So difficult was the computation of this date that the dates for Easter were worked out for long periods of years, and each monastery obtained one of these calendars. As the years were on the left side of the parchment and the Easter dates on the right, the monks began to make a brief record of any events that happened in a given year in the space found in the center of the parchment and along the margins. From this unambitious beginning we have the annals developing into longer chronicles of the events of the different years. They were written by monks, whose names we do not know, but presumably they were strictly contemporary. Unfortunately, copies of these annals were carried from one monastery to another, and the copyists were usually so inaccurate in their

The Coronation of Charles the Great

work that it is difficult to estimate the value of the variations or to know which manuscript may have been the original source.

1. The *Annales Laurissenses*, or the *Annals of Lorsch*, are so named because one of the early manuscripts came from the abbey of Lorsch, and an early German editor concluded that they had been written in this monastery. However, it is now generally believed the annals after the year 789 were written by men who either lived at the court of Charles or were very closely connected with the court. They become a veritable chronicle of the deeds of Charles, and are often called the *Royal Annals*, and critics have tried to prove that they were written by Einhard or other famous men of the time. Another theory that has been advanced is that Charles himself had them written by his chaplains, and that they were thus official annals. None of these opinions can be accepted absolutely, but in any event we can be certain that the *Annales Laurissenses* were written by prominent men who probably lived at the center of political life and had access to the best sources of information.

2. The *Annales Laurishamenses* were also attributed to the monks of Lorsch. Certain references to the monastery of Lorsch gave them their name, but it is not possible to know whether they were actually written there or were merely copied from other annals. They treat events in a very different manner from the *Annales Laurissenses*, and neither could have been a copy of the other. After the year 786 they develop into a more complete narrative of the events of each year and show a decided improvement in style. They relate military events, political and state affairs, thus giving every indication of having been written by intelligent and well-informed men.

3. The *Vita Karoli* (the *Life of Charles*) was written by

Parallel Source Problems in Medieval History

Einhard, who was born between 768 and 770, and died March 14, 840. He was educated in the monastery of Fulda, but became attached to the court about 794 or 796. He was intimate with Charles, and occupied a prominent position in public life. The *Vita* was written shortly after the death of Charles, and no one was better qualified to be the emperor's biographer. Einhard was one of the group of learned men that Charles had gathered about him from all parts of the West, of which Alcuin was the guiding spirit and teacher. His interest in classical literature led him to imitate the *Life of Augustus* by Suetonius when he wrote the *Vita Karoli*. For this reason the subject matter and form of his biography are distinctly different from that of other writers of the period. From a literary standpoint, Einhard's work is one of the very best productions of the Carolingian renaissance.

4. The *Chronographia* of *Theophanis*, called the "Confessor."

Theophanis was a contemporary of Charles the Great and an important Greek writer. He was born in the reign of Constantin Kopronymos (741–775). He was involved in the image-worship controversy, and was in prison for twelve years, being finally banished to the island of Samothrace, where he died about 817. Because of his sufferings in the cause of the Church he was honored as a confessor.

At the death of Georges Synkellos, who was writing a history of the world, Theophanis promised to complete the chronicle which his friend was forced to leave incomplete. He thus worked on the *Chronographia* ((*History* or *Annals*) from about 810 or 811 to 814 or 815. The *Chronographia* was a chronicle of world history, which was to have a great influence on the writers of history in the East and West, for it was soon translated into

The Coronation of Charles the Great

Latin, and thus became familiar to western scholars. The first part of the work is a mere compilation, but for the time of the coronation, Theophanis was a contemporary, and can give us something of the Byzantine attitude toward this event.

5. The *Vita Leonis III.* comes from the *Liber Pontificalis* or the *Book of the Popes*. There has been a great deal of controversy about the reliability of this work, which consists of the lives of the popes from the earliest times down to the fifteenth century. These biographies were written by various authors, for there seems to have been a desire to make it a complete record of the lives of the popes. From the eighth century on the biographies were probably contemporary or nearly so. The *Life of Leo III.* was probably written somewhat later, but it contains details that are not found in the other accounts, and it is particularly valuable in that it gives a version of the coronation written from the Church's point of view. It should, however, be used with caution.

6. *De Gestis Karoli Magni*, or *The Deeds of Charles the Great*, by the Monk of St. Gall.

This account of Charles was written between 884 and 887, at the request of Charles the Fat, who had visited the monastery of St. Gall in December of 883. It has been attributed to Notker Balbus; but it is not certain that he wrote it, although the style resembles other works of Notker.

This *Life of Charles*, which was written three-quarters of a century after his death, is interesting chiefly because it shows how men of later generations regarded this great hero of the Middle Ages. As the account of the Monk of St. Gall indicates, a legend was already growing up which was to obscure the real Charles. The work is filled with anecdotes and mythical tales about the emperor. Many of them were purely local and had grown up and developed in that part of Germany in which St. Gall is located. The account of the coronation shows how this event was regarded by a man of the late ninth century.

III. QUESTIONS FOR STUDY

1. What reasons did Charles have for going to Italy?
2. How did Charles adjust the troubles at Rome?
3. Did Charles actually try the pope in the council that he assembled?
4. What reasons can you find for the oath of purification taken by the pope?
5. How did Charles deal with the enemies of Pope Leo?
6. Do the actions of Charles indicate that he had greater authority in the city of Rome than the pope?
7. What reasons can you find for Charles sending such important *missi* to accompany Pope Leo back to Rome?
8. What was the pope's attitude toward Charles, and how did it affect the coronation?
9. Work out the details of the coronation ceremony?
10. By what right was Charles made emperor?
11. What evidence can you find which would indicate that Charles owed his title to the papacy?
12. From the evidence in the accounts, what do you think was Charles's attitude toward the Christian religion and the papacy?
13. How can you explain Einhard's statement that Charles was not eager to be crowned emperor?
14. What difference in point of view and what wrong information do you find in the account of the Monk of St. Gall?
15. Criticize the account from the *Vita Leonis III.* by comparison with the other accounts.

Other topics might consist of criticisms of the accounts given in standard secondary works by a comparison with the sources. The use of Bryce's *Holy Roman Empire* in this way would be an extremely profitable exercise.

IV. The Sources

1. The *Annales Laurissenses* (the *Annals of Lorsch*).

800 . . . And in the beginning of the month of August, when he [Charles] reached Mainz, he decided to journey into Italy. When he reached
5 Ravenna with his army he made preparations for an expedition against the Beneventians. After a delay of seven days Charles started for Rome, having ordered his son Pepin to ravage the lands of the Beneventians with the army. As he approached
10 Rome, Pope Leo, accompanied by Romans, met him at Nomentum, which is at the twelfth milestone from the city. After greeting him with the greatest humility the pope dined with him at this town. The pope then returned to the city, and on the following
15 day he stationed himself on the steps of the basilica of the blessed apostle Peter, with the standard of the Roman city, and crowds of pilgrims and citizens arranged and disposed in suitable places to shout praises to those coming. Leo himself with
20 the clergy and bishops received Charles when he dismounted from his horse and ascended the steps. When an oration had been delivered, while all were

chanting psalms, the king was led into the basilica of the blessed apostle Peter. This happened on the eighth day before the Calends of December (November 24).[1]

Seven days later the king began to busy himself with the important affairs that had brought him and all his men to the city of Rome, and thenceforth daily he was occupied with these matters. The first and most difficult of these tasks was the investigation of the crimes of which the holy pontiff[2] had been accused. As no one wished to be sponsor for the pope's guilt, Leo ascended to the altar of the church of the apostle Peter in the presence of all the people, with the Evangel in his hand, and by oath, in the name of the Holy Trinity, purged himself of the charges which had been made against him.

On the same day Zachary returned from the East with two monks, whom the Patriarch of Jerusalem had sent back with him.[3] One of them was from the

---

[1] According to the Roman method of reckoning time, the Calends were the first day of the month. In counting the number of days before the Calends, the first of the month was counted in. Thus the eighth before the Calends of December would be November 24th.

[2] The pope was called by various names, as pontiff, apostle, bishop, etc.

[3] In 799 Charles was visited by a monk from the Patriarch of Jerusalem, who brought blessings and relics from the Holy Sepulcher. On Christmas day of the same year Charles sent back a priest, Zachary, with gifts for the Holy Sepulcher, and other sacred spots around Jerusalem. On his return one year later Zachary found Charles at Rome.

The Coronation of Charles the Great

Mount of Olives and the other from St. Saba. As a blessing they brought the keys of the Holy Sepulcher and of Mount Calvary, also the keys of the city and of the Mount (Zion) and a banner. The king received them graciously, and kept them with him many days, sending them away in April with gifts. He celebrated the birthday of the Lord at Rome. And the number of the years changed into 801.[1]

On the most sacred birthday of the Lord, while the king was at mass, and just as he was rising from prayer before the grave of St. Peter, Pope Leo placed the crown on his head, and all the people shouted "Charles Augustus, crowned great and peace-giving *Imperator* of the Romans, life and victory!" After this praise he was saluted by the apostle according to the custom of the ancient emperors.[2] The title *Patrician* was dropped, and he was called *Imperator* and *Augustus*. After a few days he ordered the men who had deposed the

---

[1] The year did not always begin on January 1st in the Middle Ages. Different dates were used at different times and in different localities. In the present case Christmas day was regarded as the first day of the year, hence, according to most of the writers, the coronation occurred on the first day of the year 801. For the Byzantine custom see Note 1, p. 19.

[2] At the accession of a new emperor to the throne at Constantinople, an election was first necessary. This election was made by the senate, with the army and the people participating. The coronation proper was a religious ceremony in which the patriarch of Constantinople crowned the new emperor. Compare this custom with that followed in 800.

pontiff the preceding year to be brought before him. They were tried according to the Roman law for the crime of treason, and were condemned to death. The pope interceded for them, and life and the integrity of their bodies was granted to them. Some of them were sent into exile as a punishment for their most serious crime. . . .

2. The *Annales Laurishamenses*[1] (the *Annals of Lorsch*).

And in the summer he [Charles] called together his lords and nobles at the city of Mainz. When he had assured himself that peace reigned throughout all his dominions he called to mind the injury that the Romans had inflicted on Pope Leo, and setting his face toward Rome, he journeyed thither. When he had arrived there he summoned a great council of bishops and abbots, also priests, deacons, counts, and other Christian people. Those who wished to condemn the apostle himself were brought before this assembly. When the king had made investigation he was convinced that they did not want to condemn the pope with justice, but through spite. It was therefore clear to the most pious prince, Charles, and to all the bishops and holy fathers present, that, if the pope wished and should ask it, he ought to purify himself by his own will, voluntarily, and not by the

(year 800)

---

[1] *Laurissenses* and *Laurishamenses* are merely different ways of spelling the Latin name for Lorsch.

The Coronation of Charles the Great

judgment of the council; and this was done. When he had taken the oath, the holy bishops and all the clergy, Prince Charles and the devote Christian people began the hymn, *Te Deum laudamus, te Dominum confitemur*. When this was entirely finished, the king and all the faithful people with him gave thanks to God, who had preserved the apostle Leo sound in body and mind. And he passed the winter in Rome.

Inasmuch as the title of *Imperator* had ceased among the Greeks at this time and the *imperium* was in the hands of a woman, it was evident to the apostle Leo and all the holy fathers who had taken part in the council, as well as to all the Christian people, that Charles, king of the Franks, ought to be called *Imperator*. For he held the city of Rome, where the Cæsars had always resided, and he also ruled Italy, Gaul, and Germany likewise. Because God Almighty had placed all these countries in his power it seemed just to them that, with God favoring it and all the Christian people demanding it, he should have the title itself. King Charles was not willing to refuse this demand, but with all humility, and obedient to the Lord and the petition of the clergy and all the Christian people, on the very day of the nativity of our Lord Jesus Christ he was consecrated by the lord pope Leo, and received the title of *Imperator*. Then, first of all he restored peace and concord to the Holy Roman Church, and he celebrated Easter at Rome.

Parallel Source Problems in Medieval History

When summer approached he directed his journey to Ravenna, giving justice and restoring order. He then returned to his palace in France. . . .

3. The *Vita Karoli* (the *Life of Charles*) by Einhard.

Although he [Charles] regarded Rome highly, during all the forty-seven years of his reign he went to the city only four times to pay his vows and to offer his prayers.

This was not the only reason for his last visit however. Indeed, the Romans had greatly injured Pope Leo. They tore out his eyes and cut off his tongue, and thus he was forced to ask protection from the king. So he went to Rome to improve the condition of the Church, which was greatly disturbed, and remained there the entire winter. At this time he received the titles of *Imperator* and *Augustus*, which he was so opposed to at first that he said he would never have entered the church on that day, although it was a very important festival of the Church, if he had known the intention of the pope. Nevertheless, having accepted the title, he endured with great patience the jealousy that it caused, for the Roman emperors were very indignant. He overcame their pride by magnanimity, in which he doubtless excelled them, and by sending frequent embassies to them, and by calling them brothers in his letters. . .

4. The *Chronographia* (*Annals*) of Theophanis.

. . . In the same year [801] partisans of the

The Coronation of Charles the Great

Roman pope, Hadrian, of blessed memory, started a riot against Pope Leo and injured his eyesight. The men who were selected to put out his eyes were moved by pity and spared him, so that he was not completely blinded. Leo immediately fled to Charles, king of the Franks. The king took vengeance on the enemies of the pope and restored him to his seat. Thus at this time Rome fell into the hands of the Franks and continued thus. Leo repaid Charles by anointing him from head to foot with oil in the church of the blessed apostle, and, having saluted him with the title of *Imperator*, he crowned him. He also clothed him with the imperial robes and insignia. This happened on the 25th day of the month of December, in the ninth indiction.[1] . . .

5. *Vita Leonis III.* (*Life of Leo III.*) from the *Liber Pontificalis*.

. . . A few days after [the arrival of Leo at Rome], the faithful *missi*,[2] who had returned with the pope

---

[1] The indiction was originally a period of fifteen years, at the close of which the Roman government revived its tax assessments. Later it was used to reckon time. The first indiction was that of 312 A.D. The ninth indiction means the ninth year of one of these fifteen-year periods, and not the ninth period. According to the Greek calendar, the year began on September 1st, so that Charles was crowned in the year 801, which would make it the ninth year of that indictional period.

[2] The *missi* were officials of the Carolingian kings, of which the famous *missi dominici* were a special type. The men whose names are given were prominent men in the service of Charles, who were sent on a special mission to look after his interests at Rome.

to Rome in obedience to the pontifical desires—
namely, Hildebald and Arno, both most reverend
archbishops; Cunibert, Bernhard, Otto, and Jesse,
most reverend and holy bishops; also Flaccus,
bishop-elect; and Helingot, Rothgar, and Germar,
famous counts. They were entertained at the table
of the lord pope Leo, and were examining those
malicious offenders for more than a week to discover
what evidence they might have against the
pope. Neither Pascal nor Campulus[1] had any evidence
that they could report, and neither did their
accomplices say anything against him. So the aforementioned
missi of the great king seized the culprits
and sent them into France.

After a time the great king joined them at the
basilica of the blessed apostle Peter, and was received
with great honor. He called a council of the
archbishops, the bishops, the abbots, and all the
French nobles, as well as the prominent Romans
in the same church. The great king as well as the
most blessed pontiff were seated, likewise they made
the most holy archbishops and abbots seat themselves,
but all the other priests and the French
and Roman nobles remained standing. He summoned
this council to investigate all the charges
that had been made against the sanctity of the
pontiff. When all the archbishops, the bishops, and

[1] Pascal and Campulus were the leaders of the conspiracy and attack that was made on Pope Leo in 799.

The Coronation of Charles the Great

the abbots heard this they said: "We do not dare to judge the apostolic see, which is the head of all the churches of God, for we are all judged by it and its vicar. Furthermore, it should be judged by no one, according to what was the ancient custom. Whatever the chief pontiff proposes we will obey canonically." The venerable chief said: "I follow the footsteps of the pontiffs who were my predecessors. I am ready to purify myself of such false charges as have been basely made against me."

On a later day in the same church of the blessed apostle Peter, when all were present—namely, archbishops, bishops, abbots, all the Franks, who were in the service of the great king, and all the Romans, the venerable pontiff, grasping the four Gospels of Christ, mounted to the altar and with a clear voice took the oath: "Inasmuch as I have no knowledge of these false crimes, which the Romans, who have persecuted me, have basely charged me with, I say that I do not need to have such knowledge." When this was done litanies were chanted and all the archbishops, bishops, abbots, and all the clergy gave praise to God and to the Virgin Mary, the mother of God, to the blessed apostle Peter, chief of the apostles, and to all the saints of God.

On the natal day of our Lord Jesus Christ all were again gathered together in the same basilica of the blessed apostle Peter, and there the venerable, holy pontiff with his own hands crowned Charles the

Parallel Source Problems in Medieval History

Great with a crown of great value. Then all the faithful Romans, when they realized how great protection and care the Holy Roman Church and its vicar would have because of this act which had the
5 favor of God and the blessed Peter, the key-bearer of the kingdom of heaven, unanimously shouted with loud voices, "Charles, most pious *Augustus*, crowned great, peace-giving *Imperator* by God, life and victory!" This was shouted three times, and
10 many saints were invoked before the grave of the blessed apostle Peter, and thus by all he was made *Imperator* of the Romans. There the most holy bishop and pontiff anointed Charles with the sacred oil, also his most excellent son [Charles] as king,
15 on the birthday of our Lord Jesus Christ.

After the celebration of the mass the most serene lord *Imperator* presented a silver table weighing . . . pounds with its legs. Likewise, at the grave of the apostle of God, the *Imperator* and his
20 son, the king, and his daughters presented various vases to accompany this table, all of pure gold, weighing . . . pounds, also a gold crown set with large gems, to be hung over the altar, and two swords weighing fifty-eight pounds, and a large
25 vessel of gold, set with gems, . . . [the list of gifts continues].

Afterward those iniquitous malefactors—namely, Pascal and Campulus—and their associates were brought into the presence of the most pious lord

The Coronation of Charles the Great

Imperator, with all the noble Franks and Romans standing about. All were indignant about the misdeeds of these men. Campulus turned to Pascal and said, "It was an evil day when I saw your face, for you are to blame for my being in this trouble." And so, each condemning the other, they themselves proved their own guilt. When the lord *Imperator* realized how cruel and iniquitous they were he sent them into France.

6. *De Gestis Caroli Magni* (*The Deeds of Charles the Great*), by the Monk of St. Gall.

Although other mortals may be deceived by the works of the devil and his satellites, it is fitting to meditate on the words of the Lord when He commended the brave confession of Saint Peter, saying, "Because you are Peter, I will build my church upon this rock, and the gates of hell shall not prevail against it," for even in these evil and troubled days the Church has remained firm and unshaken.

Because jealous people are always consumed by envy it was generally customary among the Romans to show hostility and even to fight against the great popes who were elevated to the apostolic seat. Thus it happened that certain of the Romans who were blinded by envy accused Leo, of holy memory, whom we have referred to above, of terrible crimes. Moreover, they attacked him with the intention of blinding him, but, checked and restrained by the divine will, they failed to tear out his eyes, although they did cut them across the middle with knives. Secretly the pope had the news of this sent by his servants to Michael, emperor at Constantinople, who withheld all aid, saying, "The pope has a kingdom of his own, higher than mine, and must revenge himself on his own enemies." Then the holy pope, following the divine will, summoned to Rome the unconquerable Charles, who was in reality ruler of many peoples, in order that he might gloriously obtain the titles of *Imperator*, *Cæsar*, and *Augustus* by apostolic authority.

Charles, who was always engaged in campaigns and military affairs, although he was ignorant of the cause of the summons, without delay came with all his warriors and fighting men: the lord of the world came to the capital of the world. And when that most depraved people heard of his unexpected arrival, just as sparrows hide themselves from the sight of their master so the Romans hid in various hiding-places. But they were not able to escape the energy and sagacity of Charles under heaven, and so they were captured and led into the basilica of St. Peter in chains. There the undefiled Father Leo took the Evangel and, holding it over his head before Charles and his men, with his persecutors present, took the following oath, "On the great judgment day may I enjoy the fulfilment of the promises of the Gospel, as I am innocent of the

The Coronation of Charles the Great

charges that have been made against me." Then the terrible Charles said to his men, "Take care that none of them escape." All were seized and condemned either to different kinds of death or to perpetual exile.

As Charles remained in the city for several days to give his army a necessary rest the chief of the apostolic see summoned all who would come from the surrounding country to Rome. In the presence of all these people and the invincible counts of the most glorious Charles, who did not suspect anything, the pope pronounced him *Imperator* and Defender of the Roman Church. Since he was not able to refuse the title, for he believed that he had received it by divine favor, nevertheless he did not receive it with joy, because he believed that the Greeks, fired by greater jealousy, would lay plots against the kingdom of the Franks, or at least be more careful to make all necessary preparations to prevent Charles from suddenly coming to subjugate their empire, for there was a rumor that he intended to do this. For on a former occasion when the legate of the Byzantine king visited him, and had told him that his master wished to be a faithful friend, and that if they were only not separated from each other by so great a distance, that he would treat Charles as a son and relieve his poverty. Charles, who was not able to restrain his burning spirit, burst forth, "Oh! If that pool were not between us, we could either divide or hold together in common the wealth of the East."

Indeed, the Giver and Restorer of health showed his belief in the innocence of the blessed Leo, for even after that cruel wound had been received He made his eyes brighter than they were before, except that a most beautiful scar remained as a sign of virtue to decorate his eyelids, very like a fine thread in the white snow. . . .

PROBLEM II

II.—Canossa: From Oppenheim to Foresheim

Canossa: From Oppenheim to Foresheim

I. THE HISTORICAL SETTING OF THE PROBLEM

IN the year 1046 Henry III. went down to Italy, deposed three popes, and appointed a fourth one. From that time until his death he virtually appointed all of the occupants of the papal chair. To be more exact, he was asked to name the candidate, and that candidate was elected. In the year 1077 his son, Henry IV., was at the feet of Pope Gregory in deep humiliation, begging to be restored to the Church and his kingdom. The causes for such a profound change are numerous.

The popes whom Henry III. had placed in power were practically all of the reform party. They were in sympathy with that reaction against the worldliness and immorality of the clergy in which the monastery of Cluny played such a prominent part. Hitherto the papacy had been too often in the hands of Roman and Italian nobles, and few of the popes had had time enough to take a very active part in reform because of their worldly interests. The new series of popes, however, instituted a very vigorous campaign against marriage of the clergy and simony. The greatest cause of these evils, the appointment of church officials by self-interested lay nobles and kings, was not so strongly attacked while Henry III. was still alive. In the crusade against the minor evils he assisted them. After his death the reform party continued to control the office of pope; and one of the ablest partisans was Hildebrand, who had occupied minor offices under the popes since 1045. His aggressive nature and unusual ability profited greatly from this long experience, and when he became pope in 1073 there were few men in Europe who could cope with him as a ruler.

Henry III. died in the year 1056, leaving his kingdom to his six-year-old son. The powerful dukes, prelates, and other feudal nobles who were ever ready to seize any opportunity of gaining more power and independence had been held in submission by the war-like Conrad and the crafty Henry, but the empress Agnes, who became regent in 1057, was not able to hold them in check. She knew but little of the intricate politics of the kingdom, and in her choice of advisers she was moved more often by personal preference than by political expediency. As a result rival parties speedily formed around her. Ambitious prelates and nobles struggled for the control of the young king, and in 1062 the archbishop of Cologne actually succeeded in kidnapping him. The regency was then divided among various churchmen, while Agnes soon went into a convent. Thus the young king was left to the care of ambitious prelates who were more interested in furthering their own power than they were in properly educating a young king. His whims were indulged, and pleasures of all kinds were provided, while his education was more or less accidental and incidental. At the age of fifteen he was girded with the sword and declared king. Troubles grew rapidly around him. On a charge of treason he deposed Otto, duke of Bavaria. Bertha, whom he had married when he was sixteen years old, he refused to accept, and it was three years before he was prevailed upon to take her as his wife. (It was she who accompanied him in his journey across the Alps in 1077.) The Saxons,

Canossa: From Oppenheim to Foresheim

who had never shown a particular liking for the Salic kings, broke forth in open rebellion, which was encouraged by the other disaffected elements. The war raged from 1073 to 1075 before Henry compelled them to submission.

The papacy had meanwhile taken advantage of the party strife in Germany to free itself from all control of the emperor over the election. The College of Cardinals was established in 1059, and, though there was some opposition in Italy, the papacy had steadily advanced its program of reform. When Hildebrand himself came to the throne in 1073 he was quite ready to take up the great issue of whether church or state should have control over the election of church officials. In his correspondence with Henry IV. during the first two years of his reign Gregory assumed a kindly, paternalistic tone, while Henry answered with apparent humility. The outcome of Henry's war with the Saxons was still dubious, and it seemed that he was willing to make some concessions to the pope's demands. When, however, victory began to loom up large toward the end of the year 1075 Henry became more independent. The important archbishopric of Milan became vacant about this time. The anti-reform party there asked Henry to suggest a candidate. If Henry named a candidate he would be following an old custom; if he left it to the local churchmen and the papacy he would be in accord with the demands of Gregory. Henry named the candidate. He did this, too, for several other offices of less importance. In southern Italy also, over land which the pope regarded as belonging to the Church, Henry placed two German nobles without consulting Gregory. Thereupon Gregory sent messengers and letters to the king, threatening him with excommunication and deposition. Henry became angry, called a

Parallel Source Problems in Medieval History

meeting of his churchmen at Worms, and there declared Gregory guilty of a number of crimes and deposed him. Twenty-four bishops signed this deposition, which, with a letter from Henry, was sent to the pope. These reached Rome just as the Lent Synod was being held, and created a sensation. But Gregory calmly received them, and on the next day sent forth letters excommunicating the twenty-four German bishops, the Lombard bishops, and, finally, Henry himself. This occurred on the 22d of February, 1076. Quickly the enemies of the king took heart; two councils which he called turned out failures; the Saxons again broke out in revolt, and even the friends of Henry began to desert him. Meanwhile, Gregory had diligently corresponded with the princes and prelates of Germany; a meeting was called at Tribur on the 16th of October, and papal legates went to attend. When they came together they found Henry encamped just across the river at Oppenheim. Here the following accounts take up the story.

When Henry returned from Italy after the election of Rudolph, most of the Germans flocked to his side. Rudolph was forced into Saxony, and for a time it looked as though Henry would regain his father's kingdom. The pope did not indorse the action of the conference at Foresheim, nor did he excommunicate Henry again—not until Rudolph had won a great victory in 1080. Then he did both. In the next battle between the two rival kings Rudolph was killed, though his army was victorious. His followers quarreled about who should succeed him, while Henry seized the opportunity to go to Italy. Here he set up an anti-pope, and after three years of fighting he forced Gregory out of Rome, installed the new pope, and had himself crowned emperor. Gregory died the next year in exile. The struggle, however, continued

Canossa: From Oppenheim to Foresheim

during the rest of Henry's reign and was not fully settled until later.

II. THE AUTHORS OF THE ACCOUNTS

The accounts which follow represent practically all the source material from which the modern historian obtains his story of the scene at Canossa, and it will be found an interesting exercise to compare the narrative of a modern writer with these sources. It will be noticed that the authors of all these selections were churchmen, and that, though this was a struggle between church and state, churchmen are found on both sides of the struggle just as the laymen. The accounts themselves are characteristic of the historical writing of this period. In style they represent varieties from the literary composition of Lambert and the rhetorical touches of the anonymous biographer of Henry to the crude, brief, matter-of-fact *Annals of Augsburg*. The imitation of classical writers, the naïve exaggeration, the ingenuous piety, as well as a certain artfulness of the age, all appear in the accounts. The writers, too, represent almost all parts of the German-Roman Empire, as they do the various factions.

1. *Annales Augustani* (the *Annals of Augsburg*).

The first selection is taken from the *Annals of Augsburg*, and is typical of this class of medieval historical writing. These annals were kept by some clerk in the town, and record merely the bare statement of the important events which had occurred during the year. There is usually no attempt at style, frequently not even a regard for grammar; but the fact that they are written year by year and represent what the writer and the particular community regarded as important makes them very valuable sources of information. The items recorded by the Augsburg scribe for these two years are characteristically brief and strive to be impersonal, but the events were too stirring to hide entirely the bias which the writer so naïvely betrays.

2. *Conventus Oppenheimensis* (the *Agreement at Oppenheim*).

a. *Promissio Heinrici regis, quam fecit Hildebrando papæ, qui et Gregorius* (Promise of King Henry to Pope Hildebrand, also called Gregory).

b. *Edictum Generale* (General Edict).

When Henry was afflicted by the excommunication which Gregory had issued against him and was abandoned by most of his subjects he was at last forced to sign an agreement with the princes at Oppenheim in the month of October, 1076. This document has been preserved with both its parts and affords an interesting comparison with the agreement as recorded by the various chroniclers.

3. *Lamberti Annales* (the *Annals of Lambert*).

With literary historians the account by the monk Lambert of Hersfeld has long been the favorite description of Henry at Canossa. Even more scholarly historians have been fascinated by his dramatic and well-written description of those events, and only in comparatively recent years has Lambert been subjected to that incisive criticism from which his style and plausibility had so long kept him immune. He was not an eyewitness to the events which he here describes. His monastery had, it is true, sheltered Henry during some of his earlier struggles, and had also suffered his wrath. The people at Hersfeld followed the career of the king with more than ordinary interest. The monastery was so situated that many travelers of note stopped there, and the important communications of both king and pope were frequently made known to them. Thus, when one of their most scholarly monks began his account of the struggles of king Henry he found an abundance of material from which to construct his account. He wrote his work in the form of annals, beginning with Adam, and closing just before the election of Rudolph at Foresheim in the spring of 1077. The whole narrative presumes to be an impartial statement of events, and was so regarded for a long time. A careful reading, however, will reveal not only a wealth of information, but also an exercise of imagination unusual for his time. In addition students of Latin may detect some passages which bear more than an accidental resemblance to ancient writings, in which he was remarkably well read. Nevertheless, this account has much value.

4. *Bertholdi Annales* (the *Annals of Berthold*).

In marked contrast to the style of the preceding account is the following by the monk Berthold of Reichenau, or by some other monk of that monastery. There is a noticeable striving after good Latin words, phrases, and sentence-structure, but the result is frequently a long, involved sentence which baffles literal translation and confuses the reader. This account, like that of Lambert, is in the form of annals, and is quite as voluminous. The writer probably had better facilities for obtaining information in regard to the following events, though his bias against Henry IV. is more evident. He exhibits, too, the piety of the medieval monk and its effect on his writings more clearly than does Lambert. Remembering that neither of these two writers was an eye-witness, that one lived in central, almost northern, Germany, while the other lived among the Alps, that both wrote shortly after these events had taken place, and that both had to rely upon the statements of other people, the reader will find a comparison of the two interesting.

Parallel Source Problems in Medieval History

5. *Bernoldi Chronicon* (the *Chronicle of Bernold*).

Not far from Reichenau at the monastery of St. Blaise another monk was writing about the events of his time. This writer, Bernold by name, had been a student and instructor at Constance, and was in some respects one of the leading scholars of his time. Even though he became a monk, he still took a great interest in the affairs of the world, and the chronicle which he wrote displays a better balance of judgment than most of the other contemporary accounts. What he has to say on the Canossa incident is unfortunately brief, but it is useful in checking the other accounts. His sources of information were like those of Lambert and Berthold, and he did his writing about the same time. He was not an eye-witness.

6. *Arnulfi Gesta Archiepiscoporum Mediolanum* (*Arnulf's Deeds of the Archbishops of Milan*).

The next brief selection is taken from *The Deeds of the Archbishops of Milan*, by Arnulf, probably a clergyman of noble birth. Arnulf was a partisan of the king, an opponent of the pope; though, when the Milanese sent an embassy to the pope in 1077 to gain the pope's pardon for their association with the excommunicated archbishop of Milan, he was one of the ambassadors. This account was written in 1077, very much nearer Canossa than the other accounts, and it is a matter of regret that Arnulf, with his superior access to information, did not write a fuller account.

7. *Brunonis de Bello Saxonico* (*Bruno Concerning the Saxon War*).

Important for a different reason is the following extract from *Concerning the Saxon War*, by the Saxon churchman Bruno. He had been in the employ of the archbishop of Magdeburg, but upon the death of this patron he became attached to bishop Werner of Merseburg, an equally

Canossa: From Oppenheim to Foresheim

bitter opponent of Henry and partisan of Rudolph, the anti-king. Bruno wrote his account probably as a justification of Rudolph, and seems to have been rewarded with the office of chancellor of the anti-king. This narrative, which was written about the year 1082, is less valuable for its facts than as a representation of how the affair seemed to the extreme Saxon opponents of king Henry.

8. *Anonymi Vita Heinrici IV. Imperatoris* (the anonymous *Life of the Emperor Henry IV.*).

The next selection is from the anonymous *Life of Henry IV.*, which was written shortly after the sad death of that king in 1106. The writer seems to have been a companion of the king during those tragic last years, and his biography is the tribute of a compassionate friend. It has been conjectured that bishop Erlung of Würzburg was the author. At any rate, the writer seems to have been very intimate with the king, and his work, which is also written on unmistakable classical models, is here valuable for the light it throws upon the plans and thoughts of Henry, as well as for its strong bias in his behalf.

9. *Liber Bonithonis ad Amicum* (the *Book of Bonizo to a Friend*).

Bonitho, or Bonizo, was bishop of Sutri and a very intimate follower of Gregory. The work from which this is a selection was written shortly after the death of the pope in 1085, and, though it was addressed to a friend, it was really an ecclesiastical history for the benefit of the countess Matilda. It is an able account by a partisan of Gregory who had access to first-hand information, and as such deserves consideration.

10. *Donizonis Vita Matildis* (*Donizo's Life of Matilda*).

At a monastery in Canossa itself was written an account of the meeting of Henry and Gregory, unfortunately, how-

Parallel Source Problems in Medieval History

ever, only as an incident in the career of Matilda, countess of Tuscany. The writer, a monk named Donizo, set himself to the task of writing a poetical *Life of Matilda*, and was very much disappointed when she died before he had finished the panegyric. The original manuscript is still preserved, and in its neatness and illumination is truly an artistic production. Though the work was not completed until about 1115, it still has value for the purpose of checking up the other writers on what actually happened at Canossa. The original is in verse, and it will be noticed that even the prose translation has not entirely obliterated all of the poetical efforts of the monk.

11. *Letter of Gregory to the German princes*, January 28, 1077.

The most nearly contemporary account of what happened at Canossa is the letter which the pope wrote to the German princes on the 28th day of January, 1077, the very day after Henry had been reconciled. The pope, however, had a very definite object in writing to the princes, and was not particularly interested in setting forth a full impartial narrative of what had occurred. Together with his letter, the oath of Henry, to which it alludes, is here printed. It will be profitable to compare the legal document with the version of the oath given by the various annalists.

III. QUESTIONS FOR STUDY

1. What were the provisions of the agreement at Oppenheim?
2. Why did Henry decide to go to the pope in Italy?
3. How many persons accompanied Henry on his journey?
4. By what routes did he reach Italy?
5. What difficulties did he encounter on his journey?
6. How was he received in Italy?
7. How did the pope happen to be at Canossa?

Canossa: From Oppenheim to Foresheim

8. What difficulties did Henry have in gaining access to the pope?
9. Who arranged the meeting?
10. What conditions did Henry have to meet before the pope would see him?
11. On what conditions was he reconciled?
12. What did Henry gain at Canossa?
13. What did the pope gain at Canossa?
14. Who won the victory?
15. What were the real matters at issue?

IV. The Sources

1. *Annales Augustani* (the *Annals of Augsburg*).

A most disgraceful discord between pope and king, between bishops and dukes, between clergy and laymen. The pope, on account of his zeal for the house of God, is repudiated. At Rome the legates of the king are ill treated by the partisans of the pope. Priests are wretchedly thrown out by laymen for being married, or for buying their offices; everything, sacred and profane, is mingled in confusion. The pope, repudiated, retires to strongly fortified castles and other safe places. A conference between king and dukes at Oppenheim. The winter continuously severe, and an excess of snow from the Calends of November to the Calends of April so that the trees wither. So barren of fruits is the soil that even the seed fails. A council of the pope and dukes against the emperor.

King Henry, going into Italy, is received with all honor by the pope at Canossa, though before repudiated by a council of the dukes. After he is absolved from the ban he is honorably treated. While the king is staying in Italy Rudolph is made

Canossa: From Oppenheim to Foresheim

king at Foresheim, in an unhallowed spot on the estate of Pontius Pilate, in the middle of the Quadragesima. He, cursed with maledictions rather than consecrated, is anointed on the same day, contrary to the laws of the church. To add to his damnation, on that very day and in the same place—*i.e.*, Mainz— a great many people are killed. King Henry, returning from Pavia, is received with all loyalty. Rudolph is driven into Saxony, his partisans in arms are visited with plunder, fires, and destruction of various kinds; his unhappy and sacrilegious followers suffer devastation and death. Laymen seize the possessions of churches and churchmen; both sides plunder and burn; many are deprived of their inheritance and benefices, many also of their lives. . . . King Henry spent the birthday of Mary in Augsburg [September 8].

2. *Conventus Oppenheimensis* (*the Agreement at Oppenheim*), October, 1076.

(*a*) *Promise to Pope Gregory*. Being admonished by the counsel of our faithful followers, I promise in all things the obedience due the apostolic see and to you, Pope Gregory. And whatever slight the honor of that see or yourself has suffered at our hands, I will strive devoutly to correct. But the more serious wrongs against the see and your reverence with which I am charged I will clear myself of at a suitable time by the aid of my innocence and the favor of God, or I will then undergo gladly a suitable penance for them.[1] However, it also behooves your holiness not to ignore those things which are spread abroad about you and cause scandal to the church. Rather, remove this scruple also from the public conscience, and by your wisdom establish peace throughout the church as well as throughout the state.

(b) *General Edict.* Henry, king by the grace of God, sends the honor of his good-will to the archbishops, bishops, margraves, counts, and dignitaries of every rank. Since we have recognized, at the intimation of our loyal followers, that in some matters we have not treated the apostolic see and its venerable pastor, the lord pope Gregory, fairly, it has pleased us, therefore, to change our former sentence, and, in the manner of our predecessors and progenitors, to accord to the holy see and its recognized occupant, the lord pope Gregory, our due obedience in all things. And if we have presumed too severely against him in any matter we will gladly render fitting satisfaction. We wish, moreover, that you follow the example of our serene highness and render solemn satisfaction to St. Peter and his vicar without hesitation, and that those who know that they are held under his ban strive to be solemnly absolved by him, the lord pope Gregory.

3. *Lamberti Annales* (the *Annals of Lambert*).

When Worms had been surrendered and the

---

[1] These two sentences do not appear in all of the remaining copies of this document.

Canossa: From Oppenheim to Foresheim

bishop was assured a most peaceful position the Saxons and Swabians returned home proudly happy. They had sent legates to the pope to insure his presence on the day set for calming the storms of civil war throughout Gaul.[1] The king, for his part, realized that his safety depended upon his obtaining absolution from the anathema before the year was up. Furthermore, for reasons of his own, he did not regard it as very safe to air his case before the pope in the presence of such hostile accusers. Under the circumstances, therefore, he came to the conclusion that it would be best to meet the pope in Italy just as he was setting out for Gaul. There he would try to gain absolution from the anathema in any way that he could Once this was obtained, his other difficulties must be easily dispelled. No religious scruples would then interfere with his holding a meeting with the princes and obtaining the counsel and loyalty of his friends against his enemies. Leaving Spires accordingly a few days before Christmas, he began the journey with his wife and young son. No German of any prominence, only one man of inferior rank, accompanied him on this journey out of the kingdom. In need of provisions for so long a journey he besought aid of many whom he had

---

[1] Gaul: In none of the original accounts is the kingdom referred to as Germany. The usual expression is "Teutonici partes." Gaul might have been used to designate Franconia, but is here a term borrowed from classical literature which Lambert read so closely.

Parallel Source Problems in Medieval History

helped in his happier days. Only a few, grateful either for past favors or compassionate for his present condition, afforded him any assistance. To this state of calamity and misfortune had he
5 suddenly fallen from the very height of rank and affluence. There were at the same time other excommunicates who were hurrying to Rome with a most ardent desire to obtain absolution; but either from fear of the princes or, even more,
10 of the pope, they would not let the king join them.

The winter this year was consistently violent and inclement. The Rhine, ice-bound, remained passable for pedestrians from the Festival of St. Martin
15 (November 11) almost to the Calends of April. The vines in most places withered up, their roots snapped off by the cold. King Henry, on his way to Italy, celebrated Christmas in Burgundy at a place called Besançon. He was received here magnificently
20 enough, considering his condition at the time, and was entertained by his maternal uncle, count William, who had very large and prosperous holdings there. His reason for veering from the right road off into Burgundy was that he ascertained that all
25 the roads and approaches into Italy, commonly called passes, had been closed with guards by the dukes Rudolph, Welf, and Berthold for the very purpose of preventing his passage. After a proper observance of Christmas he set out from there and

Canossa: From Oppenheim to Foresheim

came to a place called Cinis.[1] Here he met his mother-in-law and her son, Amadeus, a man of eminent authority, extensive possessions, and very honorable reputation in these parts. At his approach they received him with honor. Nevertheless, they refused to grant him an escort through their territory unless he paid them the five adjacent Italian bishoprics as the price of the journey. This the counselors of the king regarded as excessive and intolerable. But, since it was absolutely necessary for him to procure passage in any way that he could, and since they were unaffected by any ties of relationship or compassion for his misfortune, it was reluctantly arranged, after much negotiation, that they were to receive a certain province of Burgundy that was rich in all things as the price of his passage. Thus did the indignation of the Lord turn from him persons bound to him not only by oath and many benefices, but actual friends and relatives. . . . His trouble in getting permission to cross was followed by another difficulty. The winter was very bitter and the mountains through which the passage lay, stretching far and wide with peaks reared up almost to the clouds, were encumbered with masses of snow and ice. Passage by horse or footman over

---

[1] Cinis: Mt. Cenis is one of the favorite western passes over the Alps, and Lambert here is apparently guilty of a misunderstanding. More eastern passes were usually traversed by those who went from Germany to Italy.

that slippery and precipitous descent was impossible without great danger. But the anniversary of the day on which the king had been excommunicated was threateningly near and would permit no delay in the journey. He knew that, unless he were absolved from the anathema by this day, it was decreed by a general sentence of the princes that his cause be forever lost and his kingdom gone without hope of restitution. Accordingly he procured some of the natives, who were familiar with the country and accustomed to the rugged summit of the Alps, to go ahead and in every way possible mitigate the difficulties of the trip for his party. Under their guidance they reached the crest of the range with some difficulty, but the descent, precipitous and, as has been said, slippery with glacial ice, defied any farther advance. The men, however, were ready to brave all danger by strength. Now crawling on hands and feet, now leaning on the shoulders of their guides, staggering over the slippery places, falling sometimes, sliding more, and at a serious risk of their lives, they managed at last to reach the level land. The queen and the women in attendance on her were placed on the skins of oxen and dragged along by the guides in charge of the party. Of the horses, some were placed on certain contrivances, while the others were dragged along with their feet tied together. Many of them died while they were being dragged along, more sickened, while but

Canossa: From Oppenheim to Foresheim

few passed through the danger whole and unaffected.

When the rumor spread through Italy that the king was coming, that he had overcome the dangers of the mountains and was established within the confines of Italy, all the bishops and counts of the region crowded to him and received him with the greatest honor and magnificence as befitted a king. Within a few days he was surrounded by an innumerable host. For there were those who from the very beginning of his reign had desired this advent. Italy was constantly infested with wars, party strife, robberies, and assaults of various kinds on individuals. This and every other invasion upon the law and the rights of the many by the presumptuous few they expected him to correct with the royal censure. Then, too, it had been noised about that he was hastening in great anger to depose the pope. This also pleased many, for it would afford them the opportunity of obtaining fitting vengeance upon him who had so long suspended them from ecclesiastical communion.

Meantime, the pope was on his way to Germany. The princes who had met at Oppenheim had sent letters to him urging him to meet them at Augsburg on the day of the Purification of Saint Mary (February 2) to discuss the case of the king. Accordingly, in spite of the dissuasion of the Roman nobles who feared the uncertain outcome of the affair, he hastened his departure as much as he could in order to be there on the appointed day. His escort was furnished by the countess Matilda. . . . When he had started he learned unexpectedly that the king was already in Italy. At the urgence of Matilda, therefore, he retired into a certain highly fortified place called Canossa, to wait there until he had more carefully ascertained the purpose of the king's coming. He wished to know whether the king came to ask for pardon, or whether he was wrathfully seeking to avenge the excommunication by force.

King Henry, however, had a conference with the countess Matilda, and sent her to the pope, laden with prayers and promises. With her he sent also his mother-in-law, his son, likewise the margrave Azzo, the abbot of Cluny, as well as some of the princes of Italy who need not be mentioned. They begged the pope to absolve him from the excommunication and not rashly to place faith in the accusations of the German princes who were moved rather by the passion of spite than by the love of justice. When the pope heard this message he said that it was unfitting and quite contrary to ecclesiastical law to air the case of a defendant in the absence of the accusers. Nay, more, he told them that if the king were confident of his innocence he should lay aside every scruple of fear and trustfully present himself at Augsburg on the day on which the princes had decided to come together. There, when the charges

Canossa: From Oppenheim to Foresheim

of both sides had been heard, he would receive most righteous justice on every point, without prejudice or favor, according to ecclesiastical law. To this they answered that the king would never in the world evade a trial which he knew would be a most unassailable vindication and recommendation of his equity and innocence. But, they urged, the anniversary of the day on which the king had been excommunicated was drawing near, and the princes of the kingdom who had held aloof thus far pending the outcome of this affair were growing impatient. If he were not absolved before that day, according to Palatine law, he would be held unworthy of royal dignity and undeserving of any further hearing to prove his innocence. For this reason, they said, he seeks absolution so resolutely, and is ready to offer any form of satisfaction which the pope may demand in order only to be absolved from the anathema and to receive the grace of ecclesiastical communion. As for the charges which his accusers bring against him, he will be ready to make full answer, as if nothing had been done by this agreement, when and wherever the pope may ordain. Then, according to the pope's sentence, he will be ready to receive his kingdom again if he refute the charges, or resign with equanimity if his case is lost.

For a long time the pope refused to consider it, for he feared that the king was inconstant and of a disposition easily influenced by his immediate attendants. Overcome at last by the importunities of these zealous advocates as well as by the weight of their opinions, he said, "If he is truly penitent, let him give to our power his crown and other insignia of his kingdom as an evidence of truth and as an act of penance: and, after being so obstinate, let him profess himself unworthy of the kingdom." The envoys considered this too harsh, and they urged him strongly to temper his sentence and not utterly destroy a reed, already shattered, by the severity of his decision. Upon this exhortation he very reluctantly agreed that the king might come in person and, if he performed true penance for his admitted errors, the sin which he had committed by inflicting contumely upon the apostolic chair he might now expiate by obedience to it.

He came as he was ordered; the castle being inclosed by a triple wall, he himself was admitted within the inclosure of the second wall, while his attendants were left outside. There, his royal regalia laid aside and without any evidence of royalty or display of pomp, he stood as a humble penitent with bare feet from morning to night seeking the sentence of the pope. This he did on the next day, and again on the third. On the fourth he was finally admitted to the papal presence, and after much discussion on both sides he was at last absolved from excommunication on the following conditions. First, that at the time and place which the

Canossa: From Oppenheim to Foresheim

pope should designate, he should appear before the German princes assembled in general council and should answer the charges preferred against him. There, with the pope as judge, if so it seemed to expedite matters, he should accept his decision, retain his kingdom if he refuted the charges, or give it up with equanimity if the charges were proven and he was held unworthy of the throne according to ecclesiastical law. Second, that whether he retained or lost his kingdom, he should seek vengeance on no one for this trouble. Third, that up to the day when, after proper discussion, his case had been ended, he should wear no ornaments of royal elegance, no insignia of royal dignity; he should not by his own right do anything in the administration as he was wont to do; decide nothing which ought rightly to be considered; and, finally, he should levy no royal or public taxes except for the sustenance of himself and his immediate servants. Fourth, that all who had pledged loyalty to him by oath should meantime in the presence of God and men remain free and unhindered by the bonds of this oath and the obligations of loyalty. Fifth, that he should forever dismiss from intimacy with himself Robert, bishop of Babenberg, Oudalric of Cosheim, and others by whose counsel he had betrayed himself and his state. Sixth, that if the charges were refuted and he retained his kingdom, he should always be obedient to the Roman pontiff and comply with

his decrees, and in accord with him stand forth as
the worldly powerful co-operator in the correction
of the abuses against the laws of the church which
had by a pernicious custom grown up in the kingdom.
Last, that if he falsely agreed to any of these conditions the absolution which he had so earnestly sought
would be endangered; nay, more, he would be considered as already convicted and confessed. He
should then seek no further audience to prove his
innocence, and the princes of the kingdom, thereby
freed from all religious scruples in regard to their
oath, would create another king upon whom they
could agree. These conditions the king accepted
gratefully and promised with the most sacred assertions possible that he would observe all of them.
And it was not a case of an acceptance of faith by
one making rash promises, for the abbot of Cluny,
though his monastic religion kept him from taking
oath, interposed his faith before the eyes of the
All-seeing God, while the bishop of Zeitz, the bishop
of Vercelli, the margrave Azzo, and the other
princes at the gathering confirmed by oath, over
sacred relics, that the king would do as he had
promised and would be led from his word neither
by any temporary straits nor by a change in succeeding events.

When the excommunication was thus absolved
the pope celebrated the solemn mass. When the
sacred offering was ready he called the king and the

Canossa: From Oppenheim to Foresheim

rest of the people to the altar. Extending the body of the Lord with his hand, he said, "I have for some time received letters from you and your adherents in which you claim that I occupy the papal chair
5 through the heresy of simony and that my life is spotted with various other crimes before as well as after I had received the episcopate, which, according to the canons, would have prevented all access to the sacred orders. This I could refute by the testi-
10 mony of many suitable witnesses, both of those who are intimately acquainted with my career from the very beginning, as well as of those who are responsible for my elevation to the episcopacy. Yet, lest I seem to rely too much on human rather than on divine
15 witness and in order to bring the whole scandal to short account before all, behold this body of the Lord which I am about to take. May it be for me this day the test of my innocence. May the Omnipotent God by His judgment either clear me of
20 the crime charged against me if I am innocent or strike me with a sudden death if I am guilty." With these and other terrible words he prayed the Lord to be most just judge of his case and asserter of his innocence, and then he took part of the sacred
25 wafer and consumed it. This he did freely while the people acclaimed aloud their praises to God and offered thanks for his innocence. Then, commanding silence, he turned to the king and said: "Do therefore, my son, if it pleases you, what you

Parallel Source Problems in Medieval History

have just seen me do. The princes of Germany have for days confused our ears with their accusations. They heap a great multitude of crimes upon you for which they think that you should not only be suspended from all administration of public affairs, but from ecclesiastical communion also, and even from any intercourse in secular life whatever for all time. They are especially anxious to fix a day and place and have an audience accorded them for the discussion of the charges which they bring against you. And you know best that human judgments often vacillate, and that falsity is sometimes more persuasive than truth. An untruth adorned with ornaments of words, with suavity, and by the genius and fluency of eloquent men, receives a more welcome hearing than the truth ungraced with eloquence which is often despised. Since, therefore, I wish you good counsel, all the more since you have in your calamities sought the patronage of the apostolic chair as a suppliant, so do as I admonish. If you know that you are innocent and that your reputation has been assailed with false charges by your enemies in a spirit of calumny, take the remainder of this sacred wafer and thus free, in a moment, the Church from the scandal of God and yourself from the uncertainty of a long dispute. Then your innocence will be proved by God's witness, every mouth turned against you in scandal will be stopped, and, with me as your advocate and the most vehement

Canossa: From Oppenheim to Foresheim

maintainor of your innocence, the princes will be reconciled to you, the kingdom restored, and the storms of civil war, with which it has been so long harassed, allayed." The king, astonished at this unexpected situation, became very much embarrassed, looked around for excuses, and, drawing away from the multitude, he discussed with his friends how he might evade such an awful test, which was a matter of difficulty. When he had recovered his spirits he talked to the pope of the absence of the princes who had kept faith with him in his trouble; that without the accord of the accusers the effect of such a test would be destroyed, and that the incredulous would question a satisfaction rendered in the presence of the few here assembled. Therefore, he earnestly besought the pope to defer the whole matter to a general council where, while the accusers were gathered together and the accusations and the persons of the accusers were discussed according to the ecclesiastical law as the princes of the realm had proposed, he might refute the charges. With great dignity the pope granted his petition, and when the solemn mass was ended he invited the king to dinner. And when this was ended and he had instructed him carefully as to what he must observe, the pope dismissed him with kindness and in peace to the men who had so long remained outside the walls. Furthermore, he sent out the bishop of Zeitz, Eppo, before him to absolve from their excommunication those who had incurred it by indifferently associating with the excommunicate before his absolution, kindly warning them not to occasion any stain upon the communion just newly received.

4. *Bertholdi Annales* (the *Annals of Berthold*).

1076

In the anathema itself the lord pope had, on the part and in the name of the omnipotent Father, Son, and Holy Ghost, and by the authority of St. Peter, commanded all Christians not to obey the excommunicated king thenceforth as king in any way or serve him or keep an oath which they had made or were to make with him. This not the smallest part of the princes of the realm observed, and, though they were very often called to come to the king, they refused, striving diligently to have zeal for the Lord as they knew it. Even if they had known him to have been unjustly and uncanonically excommunicated, yet, according to the decree of the council of Sardica,[1] they must not communicate with him in any way until they knew that he had been reconciled. Wherefore, fearing to associate with the king as yet unreconciled, since they could neither persuade him nor punish nor correct him, and since they shuddered to agree with him, they strove, as was fitting, to avoid him. Therefore the lords of the kingdom agreed, in the fall, to have a conference with him at Magdeburg,

[1] The council alluded to here is the church council which was held at Sardica 343 A.D.

Canossa: From Oppenheim to Foresheim

where they could by general council define what
ought to be done about the matter of such great
importance, and where they might be allowed to
serve their king and lord, when he had been admonished, turned to penance, and reconciled. When
they assembled there with no small force of soldiers,
the king and his advisors were encamped on the
other side of the Rhine at the town of Oppenheim
with a considerable gathering of loyal men, threateningly and angrily wrought up. The princes of
the realm, however, remained on this side of the
Rhine; they questioned among themselves and,
with God's assent, conferred more intimately one
with another as to what conclusion they should
reach in such an unusual matter. Thither had
come the legates of the apostolic see with letters
pertaining to this matter, by which the pope had
intrusted the bishop of Patavia, already long accepted as apostolic representative, to reconcile all
canonically, the king excepted, who fittingly came
to render satisfaction and do worthy penance, those
namely who wished to stand on the side of St.
Peter. Of these, the archbishop of Mainz with
his knights, the bishops of Treves, of Strasburg,
of Verdun, of Luttich, of Münster, the elect of
Utrecht, of Spires, of Basel, of Constance, the one
at Ulm, and several abbots, as well as a considerable host of more or less important personages who
had been excommunicated because of the crime of

associating with the king for disobedience or because they had received masses and offices from priests condemned for incontinence or the heresy of simony, were there reconciled and received into communion.

Finally, after they had spent ten days in such matters, the king, when he saw and heard that so many and such great men had yielded to the apostolic see, and that they were considering making another king in his place, pretended to yield, though unwilling and reluctant and no longer with any spirit beyond his grief, not only to the pope, but also to the princes of the realm, in all that they wished to impose on him or wanted him to observe. To them it then seemed, in addition to other things, that in the first place the see and city should be freely returned to the bishop of Worms, that the queen should leave it with all her following, that their hostages should be returned to the Saxons, and that the king should entirely separate himself from his excommunicated followers, and that he should also, without delay, send letters to pope Gregory, strongly intimating that he would perform due obedience, satisfaction, and fitting penance, and that he himself should await the apostolic answer and reconciliation, meanwhile abiding by their advice. These and all the other matters the king performed there, though not with entire candor. From thence he despatched the letters, composed as they had agreed between themselves and sealed in their presence—he, neverthe-

Canossa: From Oppenheim to Foresheim

less, later secretly altered and changed these to suit his will—to be presented to the pope at Rome by the archbishop of Treves. But the princes of the kingdom, fearing the tricks and the usual folly of the king's counselors, which they had so often experienced, likewise directed to Rome, in haste, trustworthy legates, who had been present at everything there enacted, so that the pope might not be deceived by their tricks, and to implore him, humbly supplicated through the mercy of God, to deign to come to these parts to settle this dissension. Furthermore, in order to constrain the king more perfectly to obedience to the apostolic see, they took oath before they separated that if the king by his own fault remained excommunicated longer than a year they would no longer hold him as their king. Then, for fear of the king's future wrath and vengeance upon them, since many of them had left him, without visiting and greeting him, so that he was greatly angered with them, they pledged each other aid if anything should be done against them on this account, and returned, joyfully, each to his own home.

When this colloquy had come to an end, about the Calends of November, a heavy snow, far greater than usual, began to cover the lands everywhere. This, an omen and sign of evil to come, greatly astounded not only the regions on this side of the Alps, but, which is more amazing, all Lombardy

with its unheard-of amount. In fact, the Rhine
and the Po alike, to say nothing of other streams,
were so hardened by the excessive freezing cold that
for a long time they afforded in themselves an icy
road for all wanderers as though over land. Thus
did the bitter and snow-laden winter continue with
constant cold even to the Ides of March—that is,
from the conference at Oppenheim to the colloquy
which was held by the princes at Foresheim. Finally, on that very day, the snow began little by little
to grow less, until after some time had elapsed it
fairly flowed.

The king, however, when the said conference at
Oppenheim had come to an end, remained for some
time at Spires with the supporters and overseers
whom the princes of the realm had assigned to him,
and lived like a penitent. Then, suspecting on account of the aforesaid oath that their (the princes')
treachery and cunning would be turned against himself, he collected his counselors again from all sides
and rashly disregarded the pleasure of the princes,
and, to the end that he might not be deprived of his
kingdom, he fortified himself most diligently with
all the industry and attention of his own genius,
with all the various investigations of his counselors,
and by conferring on plans together.

The bishop of Toul, and also the one of Spires,
with many others upon whom this had been imposed as a mark of obedience by the bishop of

Canossa: From Oppenheim to Foresheim

Patavia, soon hastened to Rome and gave themselves up to the pope as guilty, with due satisfaction and obedience. When these had been canonically reconciled he had them imprisoned in the jails of certain
5 monasteries in order to test their obedience for some time, until by the intervention of the empress they were released therefrom and were permitted to return home with the grant of communion, but without having their rank restored.

10 Upon their footsteps the archbishop of Treves followed in great haste with the letters of the royal embassy, saluted the pope, and presented to him the falsified letters. These the pope was unwilling to have read except in the presence of the legates of
15 the princes, so that they, who had also been present at the writing, might be witnesses at the reading. Accordingly, after these had been read, the legates recognizing the material as far other than that which had been composed and sealed in the presence of the
20 princes of the realm, protested most freely by the Lord God that it was not the same, but that it had been altered and changed in places. So the archbishop of Treves, though at first he began to defend the letters, yet at length when he had been caught
25 and reminded by these men confessed publicly that the fraud in these letters was not his, but the work of some one else whom he did not know. Thus the lord pope, together with the empress, watchfully discovered that all which this lying letter said of the

obedience of the king was not a truth from the heart but was feigned statement full of deception. Thus what the king most anxiously entreated—namely, that he be permitted to come to Rome to be reconciled with the pope, the pope was unwilling to grant at all, but with apostolic authority commanded him to meet him at Augsburg in the presence of the princes of the realm, to be heard and reconciled by him, and he sent back word emphatically enough by the legates of both parties that he would come there to them about the feast of the Purification of St. Mary if God willed it. When they had received the letters of apostolic benediction in which, as is fitting, he admonished them very carefully, especially about his escort, about other necessaries, and about the peace, they returned joyfully to their fatherland to announce the coming of so great a guest.

Accordingly, when the princes had gratefully heard what these letters conveyed, they strove with every effort to make every preparation, not a little exhilarated by the great hope of restoring the ecclesiastical religion and observance. The heart of the king, stirred with far different intention, when he found out the proposition of the pope, strove industriously, with many consultations, to meet him before he entered our territory. For he proposed either to force the pope into flight in terror of the very great force of soldiers which he had gathered

Canossa: From Oppenheim to Foresheim

together at any price or, with the help of the Romans and his other counselors whom he had corrupted with such great gifts and thus made them each his supporter, to force the pope to his wish. If that
5 failed, however, they, as warlike and angry as himself, should together fight to drive the pope unhurt from the church and substitute another after the heart of the king; and, thus elected and ordained as emperor by that pope, he would, with his wife,
10 return to his fatherland in glory; that if, he however foolishly enough planned, by all these measures he succeeded in making the pope, overcome by the threats and blandishments of the Romans, compliant to himself, he would then be pious toward him, but
15 very severe toward his adversaries.

Advised and encouraged by these and, as rumor has it, not a few other senseless proposals of his counselors, he obstinately set himself against the correction arranged by the princes and against the
20 restoration of the church and did not cease to oppress their [of the princes] magistrates in every way and to free himself entirely from them as he wished. To this purpose a certain margrave, Opertus by name, who came at this time from Lom-
25 bardy, encouraged him more than the others. This man, magnificently loaded by him with gifts and honors, was seized with sudden death near Augsburg as he was on his way to his own country. He had fallen from his horse, and thus as he died a wretch

condemned, he discovered how great a load the apostolic anathema was, although he had formerly regarded it as nothing.

The king celebrated the birth of the Lord at Besançon in Burgundy as best he could, for he remained there scarcely a day. Then after he had taken up his wife and son and also a whole host of followers, as had already been previously arranged, crossing the Rhone at Geneva, climbing and crawling over the Alps by the most difficult way, he entered Lombardy through the bishopric of Turin. There, collecting to himself also the host of excommunicated bishops, and as if to fortify their case by a sort of defensive majesty, he told them craftily that he would speak to the pope not only about the sentence of anathema on himself, but rather to have the harmful sentence over them investigated by him. They, however, on the contrary, tried to dissuade the king from calling him pope, whom they had at his command cast forth from the church abjured, and whom they had forever separated from the body of the church as condemned by an anathema. Nevertheless, they thought it fitting to yield to time and comply, since he was constrained by the bond of such unavoidable necessity lest he, as false king, should rashly annul the pleasure of the princes entirely, and thus most justly incur their opposition; but then, that is to say, after this dispensation and the address to the pope, so necessary to him, he should,

Canossa: From Oppenheim to Foresheim

together with them, labor with every effort to free himself and the whole kingdom from so sacrilegious a man; but if he did not do this he should not ignore the fact that he himself would, by the most crafty spite and arrogance of him who bore the apostolic name, be deprived not only of his kingdom and honor but probably of his life, and he should not in the least doubt that they, who had always been undaunted and prepared to go with him to death and destruction, would perish and be condemned likewise.

When, however, the legates of the king and of the princes had been dismissed by the pope and had begun their journey home, the pope, ever most ready to devote himself to his flock, at the appointed time went to the place which they had agreed upon; and there, as they had arranged, he awaited the escort for his march with impatience. But in vain; for when the princes found out about the stealthy and unexpected flight of the king over the Alps, they feared the wiles and assaults of the king; and though they were reluctant and unwilling, they ceased trying to send the agreed escort to meet the pope. So the pope waited for them some time at the castle of Canossa. But when they, with difficulty, sent word to the pope that they could not come to him in the face of such dangers, then he was very much vexed that he had come there in vain, but not giving up hope of being later able to reach the Teutonic lands for the needs of the church, he was disposed to stop there for some time to wait for such an event. Then, reflecting that the journey of the king and his counselors was not of much advantage to the church and himself—nay, that it would render the Lombards, whom he had found rebellious to God and himself, much more rebellious; that it had troubled the people of Germany, distracted by no mean schism, and greatly worried them as to what they should do about so senseless a man; and that it had greatly disturbed the whole kingdom on all sides— he placed all his cares on the Lord, as befits an apostolic man, and prayed with tears day and night that the Divinity inspire him how he might rightly arrange to settle such a great matter synodically.

Then the king, accepting the wholesome advice of his men, laid aside the plan which he had with mad anger and malice conceived against the pope, and decided, with the intervention and aid of the countess lady Matilda, of his mother-in-law, marchioness Adelaide, of the abbot of Cluny, who had himself come there after he had just recently been reconciled at Rome for having associated with the king, and of all the others whom he could attract to his side, to meet the pope and submit, yield, obey, and agree with him in everything. With this intention, though he concealed it somewhat from the Lombards, he sent messengers to bring the aforesaid mediators to himself, and he himself followed them

Canossa: From Oppenheim to Foresheim

shortly to the aforesaid castle. These, meeting the king at the appointed place, aired the matter for which they had come together at great length, and considered it in every way with the usual consultations, but I know not what tricky and deceitful promises they gave in their most careful consideration, which they were quite afraid to bear as straightforward and true to the pope, who was, in truth, most experienced, for he had long been and was almost daily dealing with such cases. Nevertheless, since necessity so demanded it, they soon came back and related to the pope truthfully, and in order, everything which they thought colored and false.

The king, following hurriedly in their footsteps, came precipitately to the door of the castle with his excommunicated friends, though as yet unexpected and without the answer of the pope or a word of invitation, and, knocking sufficiently, he begged with all his strength to be allowed to enter. There, dressed in coarse woolen garments, with bare feet and freezing, he stayed outside the castle, even to the third day, with his friends, and thus, most strictly tested by many trials and temptations and found obedient as far as human judgment extends, he demanded with tears, as is the custom of penitents, the favor of Christian communion and the apostolic reconciliation.

The lord pope, however, who was most cautious and as unwilling to be deceived as to deceive, and who had so frequently been deluded by so many promises of the king, did not very easily credit his words. After much exchange of opinion he was at last persuaded that if the king would come most promptly to confirm by oath in person, or through others whom he might name as witnesses for himself, these conditions which he would now impose for the welfare of the holy church, and should in addition consent to give pledges into the hands of those intermediaries who were present for the observance of this oath and also of the empress, who was not yet there; if he should thus bind the compact he would not refuse to receive him again to the favor of Christian communion. The king with his followers, however, when he heard this answer of the pope, regarded the proposal as too harsh; but since he could not otherwise be reconciled, willing or unwilling, he agreed to it most sadly.

At length they intervened with the pope, who agreed that the king need not take the oath; two bishops, however, of Naumburg and Vercelli, besides other friends of his who would take oath, were chosen to take the oath for him. Who, that we may commemorate this most important oath, swore in this fashion—namely, that their lord Henry, whenever within the year pope Gregory should decide, would come into peace and concord with the princes of the realm either according to the judgment or the compassion of the pope, and that

Canossa: From Oppenheim to Foresheim

neither he nor any of his men would inflict any harm upon the pope or his legates into whatever parts of the kingdom they should come for the welfare of the church, nor should he capture or kill them; and if
5 they were harmed by any other person, he should aid them in good faith as soon as he could; and if there were any obstacle in his way so that he could not meet the engagement which the pope had fixed, then as soon as possible he should meet it without
10 further delay. When this agreement had been made as before said, the king, weeping copiously, and the other excommunicates also in tears, were allowed access to the pope. What tears were shed by either party no one can easily say. When the
15 pope, not a little moved for these lost sheep who were again seeking God with their pitiable lament, had delivered a suitable address on canonical reconciliation and apostolic consolation to them, after they had prostrated themselves with fitting humility
20 and had confessed their rash presumption, and thus with apostolic indulgence and benediction, reconciled and restored to Christian communion, he took them into the church. Then, when he had made the customary oration and had greeted the king and
25 the five bishops of Strasburg, Bremen, Lausanne, Basel, and Naumburg, and many others with the holy kiss, he called the king to the place of communion and extended to him the Eucharist which he had before forbidden him. The king, protesting

that he was unworthy of participation in it, departed without the communion. Wherefore the pope not unwisely took it as an indication of impurity and an evidence of some hypocrisy latent in him, which the Spirit revealed, and after that he never presumed to place full faith in his words. But then when the dinner was quite ready they ate together at the same table and satisfied their wants with sober food; then, rising with the act of grace, they talked together about the most necessary matters of the promise of obedience, the pledges given, that the oath should not be violated, about the perfection of penance, as well as about avoiding contact with the excommunicated Lombards. Then the king, after he had received the apostolic freedom and benediction, departed with all of his followers except the bishops, whom the pope ordered to be imprisoned as suited his good pleasure. Furthermore, the binding of this oath, which remained still to be done by the friends of the king, he insisted should be performed by them. This they tried to change from its agreed form, in fear that they would soon be taken by the pope as guilty of perjury; and in order not to swear they fled in every direction. One of them, the bishop of Augsburg, fled clandestinely at night without the permission of the pope and without being reconciled to him. Thus in the first compact which they had agreed upon these mendacious men left the pope craftily deluded and deceived.

Canossa: From Oppenheim to Foresheim

About the same time that Roman[1] Quintius, who to the addition of his damnation now held the bishop of Como captive, near the church of St. Peter at Rome, thought to visit the king at Pavia, and expected the king to treat him magnificently; nay, he didn't doubt at all that he deserved to have great gifts given to himself, not only for the capture of the bishop, but also for the sacrilegious seizure of the pope. When he came to the court the king did not dare to receive him with the kiss as he was wont to greet his friends, since Quintius was excommunicated, but feigned that on account of the many important affairs which now occupied him he could not receive him as was fitting and as he so much deserved, and thus he put off meeting his friend for some days. Quintius, however, somewhat angered, proclaimed that he was being disdained and deceived until he at length extorted from the king the promise of favors and most certain evidences of a fitting reception. But on the night before the appointed day he was suffocated by a sudden deadly tumor in his neck, and without seeing or greeting the king he most quickly descended to the infernal regions, condemned to eternal death.

---

[1] This Quintius, or Cencius, was a Roman noble who bitterly opposed Gregory. At Christmas-time, 1075, he had boldly captured the pope and was carrying him off when an angry mob overtook him and rescued Gregory. He himself managed to escape and continued to plot against the pope.

Parallel Source Problems in Medieval History

5. *Bernoldi Chronicon* (the *Chronicle of Bernold*).

Already almost all the princes of the realm had withdrawn from association with the king. Accordingly, in the month of October a conference was held at Oppenheim by the princes of the kingdom, in which an embassy of the apostolic see took part. There Henry promised most assuredly that he would present himself to the lord pope at Augsburg on the next festival of the Purification of Saint Mary. For there he, together with the princes of the realm, had also invited the apostolic lord. Brother Cadalous, who had been converted from secular knighthood, brought to the conference of Oppenheim the message of the pope which task the pope had imposed upon him, when he was very ill, for the remission of all sins. When his mission had been accordingly fulfilled brother Cadalous rested in peace under evangelical perfection after he had taken the monk's garb.

The duke of the Poles crowned himself king. Very much snow covered the whole kingdom from the second day before the Calends of November of the year before to the seventh day from the Calends of April of the present year. Henry, called king, mistrusting his own case, and therefore evading the general hearing, stealthily entered Italy against the command of the pope and the counsel of the princes and met the pope before the Purification of Saint Mary at Canossa, just as he was on his way to

Canossa: From Oppenheim to Foresheim

Augsburg at the appointed day. Where, by the pretense of an unheard-of humiliation, as indeed he could, he extorted from him with difficulty not the concession of the kingdom but only of communion, but not until he had given oath that he would satisfy the judgment of the pope in regard to the charges brought against himself and that he would not permit any hurt to be inflicted upon the pope or any one in his service, journeying to and from any place. This oath, however, he did not keep fifteen days, when the venerable bishop Gerald of Osria and Anselm of Lucca were taken captive. Wherefore the pope declared in the letters which he sent to the princes of the kingdom that he had accomplished very little by the fact that he had received him back into communion, since all the simoniacs and excommunicates were no less fostered by the king now than before. When, therefore, they heard of this the princes of the realm met for a general conference at Foresheim on the third day of the Ides of March and elevated the worthy duke Rudolph as their king, whom they crowned at Mainz on the seventh day from the Calends of April, which in this year occurred in the middle of the Quadragesima. The very great snow, however, which in this year had covered the whole earth so long a time nevertheless began to melt at the election of the new king. On the day of his consecration, moreover, a very great uprising was started in Mainz at the

instigation of the simoniacal clergy as if they wanted to break into the place and kill the most upright clergy and monks. But the right hand of the Lord so protected the soldiers of the new prince that,
5 although unarmed, they lost only one of their number, while they killed more than a hundred of their adversaries partly by the sword and partly by the water. For this homicide, likewise, such a penance was imposed by the legate of the apostolic see that
10 each one had to fast forty days or feed forty poor people, yet not shun ecclesiastical communion like homicides.

6. *Arnulfi Gesta Archiepiscorum Mediolanum* (*Arnulf's Deeds of the Bishops of Milan*).

15 At the same time that barbaric throng of Teutons, foremost among them the dukes Berthold, Rudolph, and Welph, together with counts and bishops,
Cap. 8 having heard of the Roman excommunication, forthwith withdrew from the royal allegiance, having
20 nothing to do with the king. In addition, accusing him of many crimes, they held him in bad repute. Meanwhile, by the counsel of the most holy abbot of Cluny and also Agnes, the royal mother, as well as of the most prudent Matilda already mentioned, a
25 general conference was agreed upon between the king and the pope for the sake of peace and justice. And when the pope had gone out from the city on his way to Germany, relying on the aid of Matilda, he came to Italy. While he stopped there he was

Canossa: From Oppenheim to Foresheim

loaded by her with many favors and men. Henry hastily went to meet him, refusing the conference set in his own country. There was a town of the countess, Canossa by name, fortified on all sides
5 by walls and, by the nature of the place, verily an impregnable fortress. There, while the pope held court, the king coming with bare feet, prostrating himself on the ground, after many tears gained forgiveness, confirming the sworn oaths of his vassals,
10 on condition of doing justice. Thus by the great prudence of Matilda peace was consolidated, though the bishops were not satisfied and remained in strife.

7. *Brunonis de Bello Saxonico* (*Bruno concerning the Saxon War*).

15 And when they had already begun to confer about choosing a new king the Saxons wanted to choose one of the Swabians; the Swabians one of the Saxons. Over on the other bank of the Rhine the town of Mainz held Henry, all hope of holding
20 his kingdom gone. Nevertheless, he sent messengers to arouse their pity that they might accord him the privilege of making reparation, for he had been punished enough. Our party, however, absolutely refused to deal with them until he had been absolved
25 from the anathema by the papal legate. To hasten the account, they agreed to endure the humility of penance on the conditions which our party held out. When he had agreed to this our men proposed first that he reinstate in full authority the bishop of

Cap. 88

Worms, who had been long expelled from his city; secondly, that he should have letters written in which he admitted that he had unjustly afflicted the Saxons. These letters were to be looked over by
5 our men, were to be signed with the royal seal in their presence, and, thus sealed, were to be given to them and carried by their messengers throughout Germany and Italy. Then he himself was to go to Rome and, by making fitting amendment, free himself from
10 the bonds of the anathema. Accordingly, the bishop was installed in the city with great honor. The letters were written and signed in the presence of our men and sent by our messengers throughout Germany and Italy, while the king prepared in all
15 haste to free himself from the bonds of the anathema through the indulgence of the pope. But every one of our men took oath that unless Henry IV., son of the emperor Henry, was absolved from the ban by the pope at the beginning of February, never would
20 he be, or be called, their king. This oath the patriarch was the first to take, and when it was set down on parchment he placed it among the letters in his wallet. Nevertheless, he kept it better in writing than he did in deed, and, as was said shortly before,
25 he suffered a cruel punishment.

Then the bishop of Patavia, legate of the Roman see, did likewise. After them all the bishops, dukes, counts, and all the other greater and lesser dignitaries who were present took the oath. But the

Canossa: From Oppenheim to Foresheim

bishops accomplished more than the others, for they kept it among their letters. Then they despatched a legate to the pope to have him come to Augsburg early in February in order to have the case considered carefully in the presence of all. There the pope might either absolve him from the ban or constrain him more closely than before. In the latter event they might then, with the pope's counsel, select another king who knew how to rule. When these matters had been accomplished the two armies separated with great friendship and marched home, rejoicing and singing the praise of the Lord.

Cap. 89

The pope had, in accordance with the wishes of the princes, started toward Augsburg in order to reach there at the beginning of February in the year of our Lord 1077. Our men, too, were hastening there to receive him with due veneration when, lo! it was announced to the pope that Henry had entered Italy with a large army. It was furthermore reported that if he had come across the mountains with his original intention it was to set up another pope. Accordingly, he (the pope) sent an envoy to meet our men while he himself turned back with many fears to save Italy from fire and sword.

Cap. 90

Henry, however, wandered through Italy, geographically, but even more was he uncertain in thought as to what he should do, for he feared that whatever he did he would lose his kingdom. If he did not come as a suppliant to the pope and receive absolution from the ban, he knew certainly that he was lost; if he did come as a suppliant to render satisfaction, he feared that the pope would deprive him of the kingdom on account of the enormity of his crimes; or, if he were disobedient to the pope the chains of papal restraint over him would be doubled. By such worries was he torn. Yet, though he felt that he was lost and would lose anyway, he selected that course as an alternative which offered most hope. Dressed in woolen garments and with bare feet he went to the pope and told him that he cared much more for the celestial than for the earthly kingdom, and offered to accept humbly whatever penance he would inflict. The pope was pleased at the extreme humility of so great a man. He bade him, therefore, not to wear the insignia of royalty until he himself permitted it, so that the contrition of his heart might be more acceptable to omnipotent God if his vile garments bore external evidence of it. He admonished him further to keep away from his court and counsel those who were excommunicated, lest the cleanliness gained by a proper conversion with the grace of God should become uncleanly by contagion with others. Both of these conditions he promised to observe, and was legally absolved. Then he was dismissed by the pope, though not without further admonitions not to lie to God, and that if he did not fulfil his promises not only would the former bonds not be taken off, but others even more stringent

Canossa: From Oppenheim to Foresheim

would be added. So he went back to his people and began to dismiss the objectionable from his court. Thereupon they began to cause trouble, saying that if he now dismissed from his presence those by whose wisdom and courage he had thus far held his throne the pope could neither give him back that kingdom nor provide him with another. By such arguments his mind was changed. He returned to his former habits and bad counsel. He placed the golden crown upon his head and thus bound the anathema upon his heart with a grip stronger than that of iron. He held intercourse with the excommunicated, and from communion with the pious he was an outcast. It was, therefore, manifest to all that his statement that he loved the celestial kingdom more than the earthly was not true. If he had but a moment remained in obedience he would now be holding his earthly kingdom in peace and when the time came would gain the celestial to hold without end. Now, however, that he is disobedient, he will not obtain this which he loves without great labor, and will not gain the other unless he greatly changes his whole life.

Meanwhile the Saxons and Swabians met at Foresheim, but there were present also legates from other regions who indicated that their people approved whatever these should suitably accomplish in regard to the republic. There was present likewise a legate of the pope who strengthened

Cap. 91

with the authority of the apostolic sublimity all the
measures which our men took for the effective arrangement of the kingdom. From the many whom
they brought forth in the election as of proven worth,
nevertheless, the Saxons and Swabians with one accord chose Rudolph of the Swabians as their king.
But when they had to approve him as king one by one
some of them wanted to impose some conditions, to
elevate him as king over themselves according to this
law, when he had made an especial promise to them
of justification of their injuries. For duke Otto was
unwilling to make him his king until he should
promise to restore the honor unjustly taken from him.
In the same manner also many others interposed individual conditions which they wanted him to promise
to correct. The apostolic legate, learning of this, kept
it from being done, and, pointing out that the king
would be king not of single states, but of all, he regarded it sufficient if the king promised to be just to
all. He said, likewise, that if the king were elected in
the manner in which they had begun, each exacting
promises in advance, the election would not be sincere,
but would seem to be polluted with the poison of the
heresy of simony. Nevertheless, certain cases were
especially excepted which, because they had unjustly
flourished, he ought to correct—namely, that he
should not grant bishoprics for money or friendship,
but to allow to each church the election by its members as the canons command. This was likewise

Canossa: From Oppenheim to Foresheim

approved there by general assent and confirmed by the authority of the Roman pontiff, that the royal power should fall to no one by heredity, as the custom had been before, but that the son of a king, even if he were very worthy, should become king through a free election, rather than by lineal descent; on the other hand, if the son of a king were unworthy, or if the people didn't wish him, the people should have him in power whom they wished to make king. After all these matters had been legally settled they conducted Rudolph, the king-elect, to Mainz with great honor, and supported him while he was receiving the royal consecration with veneration and with might, as was soon apparent. He was, however, consecrated by Seigfrid, archbishop of the city of Mainz, in the presence and with the assistance of very many others in the year of the Lord 1077 on the 7th day from the Calends of April (26th of March).

8. *Anonymi Vita Heinrici IV., Imperatoris.*

Their [Saxons'] conspiracy was further strengthened by the addition of some of the Lombards, Franks, Bavarians, and Swabians. Exchanging mutual pledges of faith, they combined to wage war on the king from all sides. They saw, however, that while they might wage war on him they could not dislodge or overcome him; nay, his strength was as yet unassailable. In order to weaken his power, therefore, they drew up a lot of fictitious charges against him. These charges were the foulest and worst that

spite and malice could conceive, charges so foul that, should I set them down, they would nauseate me to write them, you to read them. Mingling truth with falsehood, they sent the indictment to pope
5 Gregory. It held that so disgraceful a person, better known for his crimes than by his name, was unfit to rule, especially since he had not obtained his royal dignity at Rome, that its rights in constituting kings ought to be returned to it, and that the pope and
10 Rome should, with the counsel of the princes, select a king whose wisdom and conduct accorded with so great an honor. The pope was both misled by this fraudulent representation and lured on by the honor of creating a king, which they so falsely held out to
15 him. He placed the king under a ban and commanded the bishops and princes to abstain from all intercourse with the excommunicated sovereign. Furthermore, he announced that he would speedily come to the Teutonic lands to deal with the affairs
20 of the church, and especially with those of the kingdom. Nay, he even went further. He absolved from their oath of fidelity all who were so bound to the king in order that this absolution might turn against him all whom that bond still held.
25 This displeased many—if, indeed, any one may be displeased at what the pope does—and they asserted that this deed was as ineffectively as it was illegally done. But I dare not set forth their assertions lest I seem with them to disapprove the deed of the pope.

Canossa: From Oppenheim to Foresheim

Soon most of the bishops who sided with the king either from affection or from fear withdrew from his side for fear of their positions. So, also, did most of their followers. When the king saw his affairs
5 in such a plight he secretly made a shrewd resolve. Suddenly and unexpectedly he set out to meet the pope. And thereby he accomplished two things— he received absolution from the ban and intercepted the suspicious conference of his enemies and the
10 pope. As to the crimes charged against him he made no particular reply, for, he asserted, it was not for him·to answer the accusation of his enemies, even if it were true. What advantage has it been to you to have had him put under the ban when, now
15 released of that ban, he enjoys his power fully? What has it profited you to have accused him of fictitious charges when, with his easy answer, he has scattered your accusation like a puff of wind? Nay, what madness put you in arms against your king, the
20 ruler of the world? Your malicious conspiracy has accomplished nothing, has profited nothing. Whom the hand of God has confirmed in his rule you cannot dethrone. Where is that loyalty which you swore to him? Wherefore have you been unmindful of
25 the benefices which he conferred on you with royal favor? Henceforth employ wise counsel, not rage. Be penitent for your venture and thankful that he did not rise up in his might and conquer you; that he did not grind you in the dust under his feet and

inflict that vengeance on you which would show to future ages what the hand of a king could do. At all events, O bishop, see that you do not wander from the paths of justice; see that you become not transgressors of your plighted faith. Nay, you know what the consequences will be to you.

9. *Liber Bonithonis Ad Amicum* (the *Book of Bonizo to a Friend*).

Meanwhile the venerable Gregory started with the grace of peace on his journey to Augsburg with the greatest difficulty on the march, for a most severe winter was then raging. The king, in truth, holding his oath of little account, very suddenly entered Italy. And there are those who say that he wished to capture the pope unaware. Which seems sufficiently like the truth, for Gregory, bishop of Vercelli, his chancellor in fact—he whom the princes had commanded to conduct the pope over the mountains —after he had crossed the yoke of the Apennines, heard that he had secretly come within the town of Vercelli. When he announced this to the pope the pope straightway went into Canossa, a most safely fortified camp of the most excellent Matilda.

The king, in the mean time, seeing that his schemes had been divulged, as was evident to every one, laid aside his ferocity, and approached Canossa clothed in dove-like simplicity. And, by suffering for several days with bare feet on the snow and ice, he deceived all the less wise, and from the venerable Gregory,

Canossa: From Oppenheim to Foresheim

who, nevertheless, was not ignorant of his tricks, he obtained the absolution which he sought; the Lord's sacrament taking a part in the celebration of the mass in this manner. For he made him a participant in the divine supper in the presence of the bishops, abbots, religious clerks, and laymen in this way, so that if the king had humiliated himself in mind as in body and believed him to be rightful pope, that he himself had been excommunicated after the example of Photius and Dioscurus, and that he could be absolved through this sacrament, the supper would be to his salvation, but otherwise Satan would enter him after the host. What more? When the mass had been celebrated they had dinner together. Then he and all those absolved from the excommunication were commanded to avoid all association with the excommunicate. But there are some who say that he swore to the pope his life and his limb and his honor. But I do not at all affirm what I do not know.

10. *Donizonis Vita Matildis* (*Donizo's Life of Matilda*).

Shortly after the death of her [Matilda's] mother the rumor spread through the world that the king had been condemned by the renowned pope. The brave and the powerful throughout the kingdom were indeed much wrought up, and said it was rash arrogance not to yield sincerely and graciously to the Roman see, which holds the keys of heaven. Wherefore they rightly decided to shun him until he should yield; until he should strive to regain the peace of the pope. When the king realized that he could not otherwise recover his rule he sent word to his relation, Matilda. He begged her without fail to devise some plan to get the pope to come to Lombardy from the city that he himself might seek fitting indulgence. And the pope, when he heard the prayers of Matilda, granted her request. The worthy shepherd left Rome, came to Canossa, and tarried there. Here she fittingly received him as the vicar of St. Peter, and was greeted by him. There, too, was the queen, wife of king Henry, accompanied by Matilda, and there was a great throng besides. Beyond me there became a new Rome while these things were going on. O city, to your honor, behold! With me are king and pope alike, as well as the lords of Italy, and also of Gaul, Ultramontane, and Rome, effulgent with the pontifical garland. Many wise men, too, are here. Among them stands Hugh, abbot of Cluny, who was godfather of the baptism of the king.

These lords held discussions of peace, and, though they remained in discussion for three days, there was no peace. And the king, wishing to withdraw, went to the chapel of St. Nicholas and tearfully implored the pastor Hugh to become surety for his peace. To the king's entreaty the abbot replied, "This may not be." Then he asked it of Matilda, but she also replied, "This no one may do but you, I believe."

Canossa: From Oppenheim to Foresheim

Then on bended knees he said to her: "Unless you aid me greatly nevermore will I shatter a shield, for the pope has punished me severely. Go, powerful cousin, do me this favor." She raised him and pledged him her word. Then she left him and went up to the pope while the king remained below. She spoke to the pope, crying out against the end of the king, and in the earnestly spoken words of the venerable lady he put faith. Nevertheless, the recalled king was to swear to be faithful to the holy see and to do whatever the patron Gregory willed. January this year was very cold, and there was a great deal of snow. Seven days before the end of the month the king, his naked feet nipped by the cold, was admitted to the presence of the pope. He threw himself on the cross, shouting again and again: "Spare me, blessed father! Holy father, spare me, I beseech thee." And the pope, gazing upon him crying, pitied him very much, and after having blessed him accorded him peace. Then he conducted mass himself and gave him the body of the Lord. They ate together in the castle of Canossa, and after he had taken his oath the pope dismissed him. He went to the city of Regina, where there was a great throng hostile to the pope and fearful that this peace would be made.

11. *Letter of Gregory VII. to the German Princes* (January 28, 1077).

Gregory, bishop, servant of the servants of God,

sends his greeting and the apostolic blessing to all the archbishops, bishops, dukes, counts, and other princes of the kingdom of the Germans who uphold the Christian faith.

Inasmuch as you have for the love of justice assumed common cause with us and incurred danger in the throes of a Christian warfare, we have taken pains to make known to you with sincere affection, my friends, how the king as a humble suppliant obtained the indulgence of absolution and forgiveness, and all that has happened in the affair since he entered Italy.

According to our agreement with your envoys, we came into Lombardy about twenty days before the time fixed for one of the dukes to meet us at the pass. We awaited his arrival so that we might come over to that country. The appointed time had already passed when news was brought to us that because of many difficulties, as we can readily believe, no escort could be sent us at this time. And, since we had no other means of crossing over to your country, we were very much worried as to just what we should do.

Meanwhile we learned for certain, however, that the king was approaching. Even before he had entered Italy he had sent suppliant envoys to us to the effect that he offered to render satisfaction to God, to St. Peter, and to us in all things. This promise of mending his ways and being obedient in

Canossa: From Oppenheim to Foresheim

all things he repeated if only we would grant him the favor of absolution and the apostolic blessing. We deferred this a long time. There were many consultations, and through all the messengers that passed between us we chided him severely for his excesses. At length he came in person with a few followers to the town of Canossa where we were staying. Not a sign of hostility or boldness did he show. All his royal insignia he laid aside, and, wretchedly clad in woolen garments, he stood persistently for three long days with bare feet before the gate of the castle. Constantly and with many tears he implored the apostolic mercy for help and consolation until he had moved all who were within hearing to such pity and depth of compassion that they interceded for him with many prayers and tears. They expressed wonder at the unusual hardness of our heart, and some even insisted that we were exercising, not apostolic severity, but the ferocious cruelty of a tyrant.

His persistent compunction and the many supplications of all who were present at length overcame us. We loosed the bonds of the anathema and received him at last into the favor of communion and the fold of the holy mother church. Those whose names appear below we accepted as sponsors for him. In addition the transaction was also confirmed by the abbot of Cluny, our daughters Matilda and the countess Adelaide, as well as by such of the other princes, episcopal and lay, whom we considered of use for this purpose.

Thus these matters were accomplished. Now we desire at the very first opportunity to cross over to your country in order that we may, with God's help, more fully settle all matters relating to the peace of the church and the concord of the kingdom, as we have long desired to do. For we want you, friends, to know beyond doubt, as you can gather from the mention of sponsors, that the whole matter is still so unsettled that our arrival and counsel with all of you are extremely necessary. Therefore do you all strive to remain in the faith with which you began and in the love of justice, with the assurance that we are not bound to the king in any way beyond that of having told him in words alone, as is our custom, to expect help from us only in those matters of his safety and honor with justice of mercy without danger to his soul or to ours.

Oath of Henry, King of the Germans.

I, King Henry, will, within the time which our lord pope has fixed, either do justice according to his judgment or make peace according to his counsels in regard to the dissatisfaction and the opposition which the archbishops, bishops, dukes, counts, and other German princes, as well as those who follow them in this matter, cherish against me. And if some great obstacle prevent I shall be ready to

fulfil this as soon as that has been removed. Furthermore, if the aforesaid lord pope Gregory shall wish to cross the mountains or go to other parts of the world, he himself, as well as those with him, also
5 the legates going to or from him to any part of the earth, shall in coming, stopping, and returning be secure from bodily hurt or seizure at the hands of myself or any whom I can constrain. Nor shall I place in his way any obstacle contrary to his dignity,
10 and if any one so molest him I shall with good faith aid him according to my ability.

Dated at Canossa on the fifth day before the Calends of February, in the Fifteenth Indiction, in the year of our Lord Jesus Christ 1077. Witnessed
15 by the bishops Humbert of Præneste and Gerald of Ostia; the Roman cardinals Peter of the title of St. Chrysogonus and Cono of the title of St. Anastasius; the Roman deacons Gregory and Bernard and the subdeacon Humbert; on the side of the king
20 by the archbishop of Bremen, the bishops of Vercelli and Osnabrück, the abbot of Cluny, and many noble men.

PROBLEM III

III.—The Capture of Jerusalem in 1099

The Capture of Jerusalem in 1099

I. THE HISTORICAL SETTING OF THE PROBLEM[1]

TO understand the narratives and to get a sympathetic appreciation of the characters, the pupil must know something of the history of the crusades and the relative conditions of western Europe and the East.

The crusaders, who in 1096 undertook the conquest of the Holy Land from the Turks, were uncultured Westerners, who knew little about the higher civilizations of the Byzantine empire or of the Saracen world. The years spent on the crusade meant a liberal education to these people, who, except as they may have chanced to hear tales of the magic East from the lips of pilgrims and travelers, had previously known nothing better than the crude life of western Europe. The wealth and luxury that they found were beyond all their expectations, and at every city that they captured the leaders quarreled; each was eager to obtain possession, to settle down in this wondrous land and build up a principality for himself. Thus, the religious purpose was often forgotten in the rivalry of the leaders, and it long seemed doubtful whether the crusading army would ever reach the Holy City that they had started out with such eagerness to rescue.

[1] The best account of the capture of Jerusalem in English may be found in Archer and Kingsford's *The Crusades* (The Story of the Nations Series, Putnams, New York.)

Parallel Source Problems in Medieval History

Thus Bohemond, the Norman adventurer from southern Italy, who probably started on the expedition with a definite purpose to win territory for himself with his sword, outwitted the other leaders and obtained the splendid city of Antioch as his prize. Baldwin, the brother of Duke Godfrey of Bouillon, left the main army at Antioch and established himself at Edessa. Raymond, the count of Toulouse and the greatest lord in southern France, was equally anxious to gain a portion of this rich land, but his ambition was checked at every point, and chiefly by his crafty rival, Bohemond. The ambitions and jealousies of the leaders threatened to wreck the crusade, but the people in the ranks at length grew weary of quarrels and demanded that they be led to Jerusalem. Thus the army forced the leaders to forget their selfish ambitions, and early in June of 1099 the crusaders arrived before Jerusalem. The jealousies of the leaders continued during the siege, and, although Bohemond was not present, Raymond was always regarded with suspicion by the other leaders.

Later, the Westerners who remained in the East and made it their home came to appreciate the culture of their Saracen neighbors. They found it to their advantage to cultivate friendly relations, but in 1099 the crusaders had not been long enough in the East to adopt so tolerant an attitude. They had been impressed by the wealth of the country and hoped to conquer and rule it, but they still regarded the Saracens as enemies of their religion who deserved no consideration. Firm in their belief that all unbelievers were an inferior race, they had not yet realized that they could learn much from their Saracen enemies. Thus at the siege of Jerusalem the crusaders show the same fanatical hatred that had characterized the beginning of the crusade.

The Capture of Jerusalem in 1099

Some lessons, however, the crusaders had learned. In warfare, where they were most expert and in which they were most interested, they had found it necessary to change their methods. The heavy Western horsemen had too often found themselves helpless before the light Turkish cavalry that never gave them peace, but would not come to close quarters and fight hand to hand. Such methods of fighting were new to the crusaders. They also found that the taking of the walled cities of the East was a much more difficult matter than the storming of the less scientifically fortified castles of the West. From the Greeks they learned how to besiege walled cities, and many of these ideas were used at the siege of Jerusalem. Siegecraft and fortification were greatly modified in the West by returning crusaders, who used to advantage the knowledge which they had acquired in the East.

The crusade and the capture of Jerusalem made a wonderful impression on the popular imagination of the West. In an age when fighting and the type of religion that found expression in the crusades were matters of absorbing interest, it is not surprising that an awakening Europe should develop a universal interest in this rescue of the Holy Land. The extracts reflect this popular attitude. The idea that the places where the Christian religion had found its origin could confer actual spiritual benefit upon the pilgrim who visited them was a part of the religious belief of the age. Its counterpart was the belief that relics, any articles that had been sanctified by some holy person, had a practical spiritual value and miraculous attributes. Thus the unearthing at Antioch of what was believed to be the spear that had pierced the side of Christ had been interpreted as a sign of the Lord's favor, and had resulted in a burst of religious fanaticism that had saved the crusaders from the dangerous plight

Parallel Source Problems in Medieval History

in which they had found themselves. Similar expressions of religious enthusiasm occurred at Jerusalem.

However, the spirit of the crusade was not mere religious romanticism. The cold-blooded ambition of the leaders deliberately exploited the religious feeling of the common people. The army itself fluctuated from intense piety, which usually appeared when they found themselves unprosperous and in danger, to moral laxity. The medieval man was a creature of moods. The matter uppermost in his mind received absorbing attention to the exclusion of all else. Thus in trying to understand these crusaders it is necessary to remember that they were naïve and childlike, but, although the ideals and standards of the age were very different from those of to-day, the motives that guided action were nevertheless intensely human even in the last days of the eleventh century. It is only by such an interpretation that the real spirit of the crusaders can be appreciated.

II. THE AUTHORS OF THE ACCOUNTS

The three extracts that follow have been translated from the Latin chronicles of the crusades. The writers of these accounts give the best information that we have concerning the capture of Jerusalem in 1099, for they were themselves eye-witnesses of this event. There are other narratives of the taking of the Holy City which contain additional information, but, because the authors were not eye-witnesses, we cannot be so sure of the reliability of their facts. Often they merely copied earlier writings or obtained their information from men who had been to the Holy Land; again they may have gone to the Holy Land later and heard the story of the siege there. In any of these cases they obtained their facts second hand.

The Capture of Jerusalem in 1099

One other short account of this event may be mentioned. It is to be found in a letter written by the leaders of the army to the pope in September of 1099.[1]

This letter and the three extracts printed below are the only accounts written by eye-witnesses known to be in existence, and they can thus be regarded as the most accurate narratives of the capture of Jerusalem by the crusaders. In comparing different statements, any bias or characteristic that might affect the point of view of the chronicler should be carefully considered. The writers present the attitude of different factions in the army, as well as the different points of view of the leaders and of the common people.

1. The name of the author of the *Gesta Francorum et aliorum Hierosolymitanorum* (*The Deeds of the Franks and other Crusaders*) is unknown. He makes no specific reference to himself in the chronicle. Other chorniclers who used this book (one of them saw it in 1101) apparently did not know the author; at least, they have not given us his name. The reliability of the work has been established by internal criticism—that is, by a careful consideration of the subject matter and by testing the facts given by the author by comparison with other writers. The account is in the form of a diary written from time to time on the march. The author was apparently not a man who knew the secrets of the leaders, but wrote down his own impressions and experiences, describing the events of which he was an eye-witness. He was religious, intensely interested in the crusade, and, because of his genuine and sincere effort to tell what he observed, his account is one of the best that we have of the first crusade. Apparently, the *Anonymous*, as he is called,

[1] This has been translated, and may be found in *Translations and Reprints*, University of Pennsylvania, Vol. I, No. 4, p. 10.

Parallel Source Problems in Medieval History

was a Norman knight from southern Italy. He accompanied Bohemond to Constantinople. Then for a short period he was with Tancred, but was again in Bohemond's service in 1098. Later, he became connected with Raymond of Toulouse, with whom he went to Jerusalem in 1099, where he witnessed the suffering and hardships as well as the final triumph. The Anonymous represents the attitude of the average crusader.

2. Fulk, the author of the *Gesta Francorum Jerusalem expugnantium* (*The Deeds of the Franks who Attacked Jerusalem*), was a priest from Chartres. He began his journey with Robert of Normandy and Stephen, count of Blois and Chartres; but at Antioch he attached himself to Baldwin, the brother of Godfrey, whose chaplain he became, and he is thus our principal source for the story of Baldwin's capture of Edessa. He was at Jerusalem in 1099. The chronicle has somewhat the form of a diary, and is full of the interesting observations that a curious Westerner of the time would make on such an expedition. Fulk represents the point of view of the crusader from northern France. The work is continued down to 1125, although the first part, containing the extract that describes the capture of Jerusalem, was probably written not later than 1105.

3. The *Historia Francorum qui Ceperunt Jerusalem* (*The History of the Franks who Captured Jerusalem*), by Raymond of Agiles, although the work of an eye-witness and the longest, deserves more cautious use. The author was a priest, like Fulk, and went on the crusade as the chaplain of Raymond (count of Toulouse), who led the crusaders from southern France. The account was written later than the others, probably about 1112. Count Raymond received favorable treatment at the hands of his chaplain, but this priest, who was canon of Puy, had personal rea-

The Capture of Jerusalem in 1099

sons for writing a history of the crusade. He was one of the men who helped to find the holy lance at Antioch. The enemies of Count Raymond, because he made every possible use of this relic, charged him with fraud, and his chaplain tried to vindicate both his master and himself by writing a history of the crusade. Thus, although his information was obtained first hand, our chronicler is biased and, furthermore, on the defensive. In any case where his information might be colored by such prejudice, careful comparison should be made with the other writers.

III. QUESTIONS FOR STUDY

1. Describe the fortification of Jerusalem in 1099.
2. What was the location of the different leaders during the siege?
3. What changes were made in the plan of attack during the siege? What reasons can be found for such changes?
4. Describe the first assault made by the crusaders.
5. How was the progress of the siege delayed by the lack of provisions and the poor water supply?
6. Describe the fight that Raymond Piletus had, on his march to Joppa.
7. What part did the fleet and Genoese sailors have in the siege?
8. What evidence of dissension and lack of harmony in the crusading army is to be found in the extracts?
9. By what means was harmony established among the crusaders?
10. Discuss the use of siege towers.
11. What machines and siege devices were used to obtain an entrance into the city?
12. What methods did the Turks use to defend the city?
13. Describe the first attack on the city. Try to give date, and tell why it failed.
14. Describe the final attack that resulted in the Franks entering the city. What was the date?

Parallel Source Problems in Medieval History

15. What part did Raymond have in the siege?
16. What resistance did the crusaders encounter after they had forced their way into the city?
17. Describe the fight at the temple of Solomon.
18. How did the crusaders treat the inhabitants and defenders of the city?
19. Describe the sacking of the city.
20. In what ways do the chroniclers illustrate the general attitude of Westerners toward the Mohammedans?
21. What can you say of the piety of the crusaders?
22. Can you show that people in the year 1099 believed in miracles?
23. How long did the siege of Jerusalem last?
24. How was the capture of the city celebrated?
25. How does the importance of the capture of Jerusalem, in the estimation of the chroniclers, show the general Western attitude toward the crusade?

IV. The Sources

1. The *Gesta Francorum et aliorum Hierosolymitanorum* (*The Deeds of the Franks and other Crusaders*), by an anonymous author.

Rejoicing and exulting, we reached the city of Jerusalem on Tuesday, June 6th, and began to besiege the city in a marvelous manner. Robert, the Norman, located himself on the north side, near the church of St. Stephen,[1] which was built on the very spot where that first martyr won eternal happiness by being stoned in Christ's name. Next to the Norman duke, Robert, count of Flanders, stationed his contingent, while duke Godfrey and Tancred prepared to attack the city from the west.[2] The count of St. Ægidius located himself on the south, on Mount Zion, near the church of St. Mary,

---

[1] The church of St. Stephen was built on the spot where Stephen was supposed to have been stoned. The church that the crusaders found in ruins was built by the Greeks about the eighth century.

[2] Tancred was the nephew of Robert Guiscard, the Norman ruler of southern Italy. With Bohemond, the oldest son of Robert, he led the crusading army from southern Italy. Raymond, count of Toulouse, was also count of St. Gilles, duke of Narbonne, and marquis of Provence. He was also called count of St. Ægidius. Raymond was the most powerful lord in southern France.

the mother of the Lord, where Christ once supped with His disciples.

On the third day some of our men, namely Raymond Piletus and Raymond of Taurina, went out on a foraging expedition. They encountered a force of two hundred Arabs, and the soldiers of Christ fought these unbelievers. With the Lord's help, they fought so valiantly that they killed many of the enemy and captured thirty horses. On the first Monday after our arrival we made an attack on the city, and so bravely did we fight that if scaling ladders had been ready for our use the city would most certainly have fallen into our hands. As it was, we pulled down the outer wall and placed one ladder against the main wall, so that some of our men ascended and fought hand to hand with swords and lances against the Saracen defenders of the city. Many of our men were killed in this attack, but the enemy lost more heavily.

However, for a period of ten days we were not able to buy bread at any price, until a messenger arrived announcing the arrival of our ships. We also suffered greatly from thirst. In fear and terror we were forced to water our horses and other animals at a distance of six miles from camp. The Spring of Siloam,[1] at the foot of Mount Zion, sustained us.

When the messenger arrived from our ships, the leaders took counsel and decided that armed men

[1] See note 3, p. 109.

The Capture of Jerusalem in 1099

should be sent to guard the ships and sailors at the port of Joppa. So one hundred men from the army of Raymond, count of St. Ægidius, under Raymond Piletus, Archardus of Montemerlus and William of Sabram, left camp in the early dawn and started confidently toward Joppa. Thirty of these knights separated themselves from the rest of the band and met seven hundred Arabs, Turks, and Saracens from the army of the Emir. The soldiers of Christ boldly attacked the enemy, but, as they were greatly outnumbered, they were soon surrounded; Archardus and some of the poor footmen were killed.[1] While this band was completely surrounded and all believed that they could not escape death, a messenger was sent to Raymond Piletus who said, "Why do you stand here with these knights? Lo, all of our men are in serious danger from the Arabs, Turks, and Saracens, and may all be dead by this time. Hasten to them and aid them." As soon as they heard this our men hastened to the scene of battle. The pagans, when they saw the rest of our knights approach, formed themselves into two lines. Our men rushed upon the unbelievers, shouting the name of Christ, each determined to bring down his man. The enemy soon realized that they would not be

[1] The knights were always accompanied by foot soldiers, so the numerical strength of this band was larger than the number of knights would indicate. In the crusading battles the footmen outnumbered the horsemen 2, 3, 4, and even 7 to 1. The personal attendant of a knight was a squire.

able to withstand the bravery of the Franks, so they turned their backs and fled in terror. They were pursued for a distance of six miles. Many of the enemy were killed, and one man, whom they regarded as a very important person, was taken alive. One hundred and three horses were captured.

During this siege we were so distressed with thirst that we were forced to carry water a distance of six miles in the skins of cattle and wild oxen, and between fetid water and barley bread we were daily in great want and suffering. Moreover, the Saracens hid in ambush at the watering places and either killed and wounded our animals or drove them away to caverns and caves in the hills.

At length our leaders decided to beleaguer the city with siege machines, so that we might enter and worship the Saviour at the Holy Sepulcher. Two wooden towers and many other siege machines were constructed.[1] Duke Godfrey made a wooden tower and other siege devices, and count Raymond did the same, although it was necessary to bring the wood from a considerable distance. However, when the Saracens saw our men engaged in this work they greatly strengthened the fortifications of the city by

---

[1] The siege tower was made of wood and was moved by wheels or rollers. The tower usually had two or more stories. In the lower story was a ram to batter holes in the wall. At the top were archers and various engines that discharged stones and other missiles. A drawbridge was also attached to the tower which could be lowered to the wall when the tower had been moved close enough.

The Capture of Jerusalem in 1099

increasing the height of the turrets at night. On a certain Sabbath night, after the leaders had decided which parts of the wall were weakest, they dragged the towers and the machines to the eastern side of the city. The tower and machines were erected, equipped, and made ready for use during Sunday, Monday, and Tuesday. The count of St. Ægidius erected his tower on the plain to the south of the city.

While all this was going on our water supply was so limited that no one could buy enough water for one denarius[1] to satisfy his thirst. Both night and day, on Wednesday and Thursday, we made a determined attack on the city from all sides. However, before we made this assault on the city, the bishops and priests persuaded all by exhorting and preaching to honor the Lord by marching around Jerusalem in a great procession, and to prepare for battle by prayer, fasting, and almsgiving. Early Saturday morning we again attacked the city on all sides, but, as the assault was unsuccessful, we were all discouraged and fearful. But when that hour approached on which our Lord Jesus Christ deigned to suffer on the cross for us our knights began to fight bravely in one of the towers—namely, the party with duke Godfrey and his brother, count Eustace. One of our knights, named Lethold, clambered up the wall of

[1] A coin that was used most commonly in western Europe at this time. It is impossible to say what the purchasing value was.

the city, and no sooner had he ascended than the
defenders fled from the walls and through the city.
Our men followed, killing and slaying even to the
temple of Solomon, where the slaughter was so great
that our men waded in blood up to their ankles.

Raymond approached the city from the south,
but he was unable to move his tower close to the
wall because of a deep ditch. So he announced that
any one who should carry three stones to the moat
would receive one denarius, but notwithstanding
this reward, the work of filling the ditch required
three days and three nights. The tower was at last
moved up to the wall, but the men defending this
portion of the wall fought desperately with stones
and fire. When the count heard that the Franks
were already in the city, he said to his men, "Why
do you loiter? Lo, the Franks are even now within
the city." The Emir, who commanded in the tower
of St. David, surrendered and opened that gate at
which the pilgrims had always been accustomed to
pay tribute. But this time the pilgrims entered the
city to pursue and kill the Saracens up to the temple
of Solomon, where the enemy gathered in force; and
the battle raged throughout the day, so that the
temple was covered with blood. When the pagans
were unable to resist longer, our men seized great
numbers, both men and women, either killing them
or keeping them as captives, as they wished. On
the roof of the temple a great number of pagans of

The Capture of Jerusalem in 1099

both sexes had assembled, and these were taken under the protection of Tancred and Gaston of Beert. Afterward, the army scattered throughout the city and took possession of the gold and silver, the horses and mules, and the houses full of loot for all.

Later, all of our people went to the Sepulcher of our Lord, rejoicing and weeping for joy, and they rendered up the offering that they owed. In the morning some of our men cautiously ascended to the roof of the temple and massacred many of the Saracens, both men and women, with their swords; the remainder sought death by jumping down into the temple. When Tancred heard of this he was filled with anger.[1]

2. The *Gesta Francorum Jerusalem expugnantium* (*The Deeds of the Franks who Attacked Jerusalem*), by Fulk of Chartres.

On the seventh of June[2] the Franks besieged Jerusalem. The city is located in a mountainous region, which is lacking in rivers, woods, and springs, except the Fountain of Siloam, where there is plenty of water, but it empties forth only at certain intervals.[3] This fountain empties into the valley, at

---

[1] Tancred apparently wished to sell these people into slavery.

[2] The Anonymous says (p. 103) that the crusaders arrived at Jerusalem on Tuesday, June 6, in 1099. June 6th would be on Monday. The different chroniclers vary as to the date.

[3] The Spring of Siloam was intermittent, and the water flowed less frequently in the summer than in the spring. In the interior of the rock there is a natural reservoir, in which the water collected. A passage connects this reservoir with the outer basin, and when the water rose to a certain height this passage acted as a siphon.

the foot of Mount Zion, and flows into the course of
the brook of Kedron, which, during the winter, flows
through the valley of Jehosaphat. There are many
cisterns, which furnish abundant water within the
city. When filled by the winter rains and well cared
for, they offer both men and beasts an unfailing
supply at all times. Moreover, the city is laid out
most beautifully, and cannot be criticized for too
great length or as being disproportionately narrow.
On the west is the tower of David, which is flanked
on both sides by the broad wall of the city. The
lower half of the wall is solid masonry, of square
stones and mortar, sealed with molten lead. So
strong is this wall that, if fifteen or twenty men
should be well supplied with provisions, they would
never be taken by any army. . . .

When the Franks saw how difficult it would be to
take the city, the leaders ordered scaling ladders to
be made, hoping that by a brave assault it might
be possible to surmount the walls by means of
ladders and thus take the city, God helping. So the
ladders were made, and on the day following the
seventh,[1] in the early morning, the leaders ordered
the attack, and, with the trumpets sounding, a
splendid assault was made on the city from all sides.
The attack lasted till the sixth hour, but it was discovered that the city could not be entered by the use

[1] This would be the 8th of June according to Fulk. According to the Anonymous, an attack was made on Monday, the 13th.

The Capture of Jerusalem in 1099

of ladders, which were few in number, and sadly we ceased the attack.

Then a council was held, and it was ordered that siege machines should be constructed by the artisans, so that by moving them close to the wall we might accomplish our purpose, with the aid of God. This was done.

In the mean time, while we did not suffer because of any lack of meat or bread, our men and their animals were unable to obtain a sufficient supply of drinking water, for, as I have said, the region is dry and without streams of water. Accordingly, it was necessary to bring water to camp in the skins of animals, from places four or five miles distant.

Moreover, the machines were being prepared for the attack, rams,[1] and hurling machines.[2] Among other siege devices a wooden tower was constructed from small timbers, for we had a very small supply of wood. According to a command that was issued, the parts of this tower were carried by night to a

---

[1] The ram was a large beam or log, which was suspended by ropes or chains from solid perpendicular beams. When drawn back it was allowed to swing against the wall. It was necessary to cover the men who worked the ram with some kind of protection, as the defenders dropped stones from the top of the wall. By the use of the ram the wall was shaken down or a hole was made through it.

[2] There were various kinds of engines for hurling stones or shooting javelins. Ropes or cords were so twisted that when suddenly released they hurled a stone or other missile. Other machines were like large crossbows, and shot javelins and stones. The petraria was a machine which hurled stones as missiles. The tormentum was an engine operated by the use of twisted cords, by torsion.

corner of the city. In the morning it was very quickly set up and equipped with petrariæ and other machines, at a safe distance from the wall. When the tower had been put together and had been
5 covered with hides, it was moved nearer to the wall. Then knights, few in number, but brave, at the sound of the trumpet, took their places in the tower and began to shoot stones and arrows. The Saracens defended themselves vigorously, and, with slings,
10 very skilfully hurled back burning firebrands, which had been dipped in oil and fresh fat. Many on both sides, fighting in this manner, often found themselves in the presence of death.

On the other side of the city from Mount Zion,
15 a great attack was also made on the city by Raymond and his men, where machinery was likewise used. However, on the side where duke Godfrey, Robert, count of Normandy, and Robert of Flanders were fighting, the battle was fiercest. Such was the work
20 of that day. On the following day the work again began at the sound of the trumpet, and to such purpose that the rams, by continual pounding, made a hole through one part of the wall. The Saracens suspended two beams before the opening, supporting
25 them by ropes, so that by piling stones behind them they would make an obstacle to the rams. However, what they did for their own protection became, through the providence of God, the cause of their own destruction. For, when the tower was moved

The Capture of Jerusalem in 1099

nearer to the wall, the ropes that supported the beams were cut; from these same beams the Franks constructed a bridge, which they cleverly extended from the tower to the wall. About this time one of the towers in the stone wall began to burn, for the men who worked our machines had been hurling firebrands upon it until the wooden beams within it caught fire. The flames and smoke soon became so bad that none of the defenders of this part of the wall were able to remain near this place. At the noon hour on Friday, with trumpets sounding, amid great commotion and shouting "God help us," the Franks entered the city. When the pagans saw one standard planted on the wall, they were completely demoralized, and all their former boldness vanished, and they turned to flee through the narrow streets of the city. Those who were already in rapid flight began to flee more rapidly.

Count Raymond and his men, who were attacking the wall on the other side, did not yet know of all this, until they saw the Saracens leap from the wall in front of them. Forthwith, they joyfully rushed into the city to pursue and kill the nefarious enemies, as their comrades were already doing. Some Saracens, Arabs, and Ethiopians took refuge in the tower of David, others fled to the temples of the Lord and of Solomon. A great fight took place in the court and porch of the temples, where they were unable to escape from our gladiators. Many fled to the roof of the temple of Solomon, and were shot with arrows, so that they fell to the ground dead. In this temple almost ten thousand were killed. Indeed, if you had been there you would have seen our feet colored to our ankles with the blood of the slain. But what more shall I relate? None of them were left alive; neither women nor children were spared.

This may seem strange to you. Our squires and poorer footmen discovered a trick of the Saracens, for they learned that they could find byzants[1] in the stomachs and intestines of the dead Saracens, who had swallowed them. Thus, after several days they burned a great heap of dead bodies, that they might more easily get the precious metal from the ashes. Moreover, Tancred broke into the temple of the Lord and most wrongfully stole much gold and silver, also precious stones, but later, repenting of his action, after everything had been accounted for, he restored all to its former place of sanctity. . . .

The carnage over, the crusaders entered the houses and took whatever they found in them. However, this was all done in such a sensible manner that whoever entered a house first received no injury from any one else, whether he was rich or poor. Even though the house was a palace, whatever he found there was his property. Thus many poor men became rich.

Afterward, all, clergy and laymen, went to the

[1] The byzant, or bezant, was a gold coin of the Byzantine empire.

The Capture of Jerusalem in 1099

Sepulcher of the Lord and His glorious temple, singing the ninth chant. With fitting humility, they repeated prayers and made their offering at the holy places that they had long desired to visit. . . .

It was the eleven hundredth year of our Lord, if you subtract one, when the people of Gaul took the city. It was the 15th day of July when the Franks in their might captured the city. It was the eleven hundredth year minus one after the birth of our Lord, the 15th day of July in the two hundred and eighty-fifth year after the death of Charles the Great and the twelfth year after the death of William I. of England.

3. The *Historia Francorum qui Ceperunt Jerusalem* (*The History of the Franks who Captured Jerusalem*), by Raymond of Agiles, canon of Puy.

The duke [Godfrey] and the count of Flanders besieged the city from the north side, while the count of Normandy stationed his men in the space between the church of St. Stephen, which is located at the center of the northern wall of the city, and the angular tower, the one next to the tower of David. The count [Raymond] and his army prepared to besiege the city on the west, occupying the space between the duke and the foot of Mount Zion. However, because a ravine in the center of this space made it impossible to cross the plain and storm the wall, the count wished to move his camp and change his position. One day, while he was reconnoitering, he came to Mount Zion and saw the church which is located on the mount. When he heard of the miracles that Christ had performed there he said to his leaders and companions, "If we neglect to take this sacred offering, which the Lord has so graciously offered us, and the Saracens occupy this hill, what will become of us? Suppose that on account of our negligence they should destroy and pollute this church? Who knows that God may not be giving us this opportunity to test our regard for Him? I know one thing that is certain: unless we carefully protect this sacred spot, the Lord will not give us possession of the Holy Places within the city." And so count Raymond, against the wishes of the leaders of his army, ordered his tents to be moved to Mount Zion. Because of his action he incurred the displeasure of the leaders, who refused to move their tents or to change their guards during the night; each stayed where he had first pitched his tent, with the exception of a few who accompanied the count. However, by offering great financial inducements, the count was able to persuade such knights and footmen as daily served under his command to follow him.

This church is sacred because it contains the tombs of the kings David and Solomon as well as that of the first martyr, Stephen. Moreover, the most blessed virgin, Mary, visited this church during her lifetime; the Lord supped there, and, after rising from the dead, appeared there to His disciples and

The Capture of Jerusalem in 1099

Thomas. On this spot, also, the disciples were filled with the Holy Spirit.[1]

Now, when the arrangements for the siege had been completed, it happened one day that some of the leaders of the army met a hermit on the Mount of Olives, who said to them, "If you will storm the city to-morrow, till the ninth hour [3 P.M.], the Lord will deliver it into your hands." They replied, "But we do not have the necessary machinery for storming the walls." The hermit replied: "God is powerful. If He wills, He will scale the walls with ladders made of rushes. The Lord aids those who labor for the Truth." So, with such machinery as could be constructed during the night, an attack was made on the city in the early morn, and it lasted till the third hour [9 A.M.]. The Saracens were compelled to retreat behind the inner walls, for the outer wall was broken down by our men, and some of them even climbed to the top of the inner wall. The city would undoubtedly have been captured at that time if the attack had not become confused and if our men had not become discouraged; moreover, we lost many men. On the next day no attack was attempted.

After this the whole army scattered itself throughout the surrounding country to collect provisions,

---

[1] The church of Zion, or St. Mary, was rebuilt afterward by the crusaders in 1130. The Coenaculum was supposed to be the room of the Last Supper. The tomb of David was also there. Raymond gives other reasons for the sanctity of this church.

and nothing was even said of the necessity of preparing the machines that were needed to capture the city; each man was interested only in his mouth and stomach, and, what was worse, they did not even ask the Lord to free them from such great and manifold evils, and they were afflicted even unto death. Just before our arrival the Saracens had filled up the springs, destroyed the cisterns, and dammed up the brooks from the springs. . . . Thus water was obtained with great difficulty. There is a certain fountain at the foot of Mount Zion, which is called the Pool of Siloam; indeed, it is a large spring, but the water flows forth only once in three days, and the natives say that formerly it emptied itself only on Saturdays; the rest of the week it remained stagnant. We are ignorant of the explanation of this, except that the Lord willed that it should be so.[1] However, when, as we have said, the water did flow forth to us on the third day, there was such great crowding and haste to drink, that both men and cattle rushed toward the water and many of our animals were killed. Thus the pool was filled with the crowd and with the bodies of the dead animals. The bravest, fighting in a struggle of death, forced their way to the very opening in the rocks through which the water flowed, while the weak got only the water which had already been contaminated. Many sick people dragged themselves to the fountain and, with

---

[1] See note 3, p. 109.

The Capture of Jerusalem in 1099

their throats so parched that they were unable to make a sound, they stretched their hands in mute appeal toward those who had water. In the field were many horses, mules, and cattle without strength enough to move, and because of thirst they died in their tracks. Throughout camp the stench of the dead bodies was most sickening. Because of such affliction it was necessary to fetch water a distance of two or three leagues, also to drive the cattle to such distant watering places. When the Saracens noted that our people were going to the watering places through the dangerous passes in the hills unarmed, they lay in wait for them in ambush. They killed whom they wished and drove away the flocks and herds. The situation was so bad that when any one brought foul water to camp in vessels he was able to get any price that he cared to ask, and if any one wished to get clear water, for five or six nummi[1] he could not obtain enough to satisfy his thirst for a single day. Nothing, or very little, was said about wine at this time; people talked about the heat, the dust, and the wind, and in this way they aggravated their suffering from thirst, as though this was not bad enough in itself. But why say so much about these troubles? Few remembered the Lord, for they paid slight attention either to such works as were needed to capture the city or to win the Lord's favor. . . .

[1] The nummus was a Byzantine coin.

Parallel Source Problems in Medieval History

Meanwhile, messengers came to camp, announcing that our ships had arrived at Joppa and that the sailors demanded that a guard should be sent to hold the tower of Joppa and give them protection at the port, for the town of Joppa had been destroyed except the castle, and that was nearly in ruins, with the exception of one tower. However, the harbor is there, and it is the one nearest to Jerusalem, being about one day's journey distant. All of our people rejoiced when they heard the news of our sailors, and they sent out count Galdemarus, called Carpinellus, accompanied by twenty knights and forty footmen. Later, he was followed by Raymond Piletus with fifty knights and William of Sabram with his followers.

As Galdemarus and his contingent approached the plains that are on this side of Ramla, he encountered a force of four hundred Arabs and two hundred Turks. Galdemarus arranged his men for battle so as to use his small number to the best advantage, placing his archers in front. Then he boldly advanced upon the enemy, trusting in the aid of the Lord. The enemy thought that they would be able to crush this band and rushed upon it, circling about them, shooting arrows at them. Three or four of Galdemarus's knights were killed, including Achardus of Montemerlus, a most honorable man; others were wounded; all of this was done by the arrows of the enemy. However, many of the enemy were also

The Capture of Jerusalem in 1099

killed. Nevertheless, not on account of all this did the fight slacken, nor did our brave men despair of the mercy of God, but, oppressed by wounds and death itself, they stood up to their enemies the more fiercely, the more that they suffered from them. But when our leaders, more from weariness than from fear, wished to retire from the fighting line, a cloud of dust was seen approaching. Raymond Piletus was rushing headlong into the fight with his men. Moreover, his men raised so much dust that to the enemy his force seemed much larger than it really was. Thus, by the grace of God, our men were released; the enemy scattered and fled, two hundred of them were killed, and much plunder was taken. It is the custom of this people, when they flee and are hard pressed by the enemy, first to throw away their arms, then their clothes, and lastly their saddle bags. Thus it happened in this fight that our few knights killed until they were worn out, but were also able to obtain the spoil of all, even of those whom they did not kill.

After the pursuit was over our men assembled, divided the spoil, and then marched on to Joppa. The sailors received them with great joy, and felt so secure after their arrival that they forgot their ships and neglected to place watches on the sea, but entertained the crusaders with a feast of bread, wine, and fish from their ships. However, the sailors, careless of their security, failed to post lookouts for the night, and in the darkness were suddenly surrounded by enemies from the sea. When dawn came they realized that the enemy was too strong to be resisted, and they abandoned their ships, saving whatever they could. Thus our knights returned to Jerusalem after winning one battle and losing another. However, one of our ships, which was heavily laden, when it was seen that the rest of the ships were surrounded by the enemy's fleet, by the use of oars and sail made its escape to Laodicæa and told our friends at that port what had been happening at Jerusalem. From signs, sent to us by the Lord, we knew that we had deserved this misfortune, for we had despaired of the mercy of God and had denied our faith. So we went to the plain of the river Jordan, collected palms, and were baptized in its waters. . . .

About this time a public assembly was held, for the leaders of the army were quarreling with each other. There was dissatisfaction because Tancred had occupied Bethlehem and had placed his standard over the church of the Nativity as though it was an ordinary house. (The question of electing a king of Jerusalem was also discussed, but the election was postponed till the eighth day after the city should be captured. This was the chief cause of trouble among the leaders.) Not in this matter alone, but in other ways, our affairs did not prosper, and the troubles of the people increased every day. Nevertheless, the merciful and propitious Lord, lest our enemies should

The Capture of Jerusalem in 1099

insult His law and say "Where is their God?" had shown us through the bishop of Puy, the lord Adhemar, how we could placate His anger and obtain His mercy.[1] For the benign Lord had sent His messengers to us, but because they were our brothers we had not heeded them. Therefore, the bishop [Adhemar] appeared before Peter Desiderius, saying: "Speak to the princes and all the people, and tell them you have come from distant lands to worship the Lord and you are His army. Therefore, let us be purged from our uncleanliness, and let each one turn from his evil ways. Then praying and fasting, let every one march around Jerusalem barefooted. If you do this and then make a great attack on the city on the ninth day, it will be captured. If you do not, all the evils that you have suffered will be multiplied." When the priest had said this to William Ugo, the brother of the bishop, to his lord, count Ysoardus, and to certain of the clergy, they assembled the princes and the people and addressed them: "Brothers, you know why we undertook this expedition, and what we have suffered, and that we are acting negligently, in that we are not constructing the machines that are needed to capture the city. Likewise we are not careful to reconcile the Lord to

---

[1] Until his death, August 1, 1098, Adhemar, bishop of Puy, who was the representative of the pope and had supervision of the entire crusade, had been able to play the part of mediator. After he died there was no one to reconcile the two factions headed by Raymond of Toulouse and Bohemond. Hence this reference to Adhemar.

us, for we offend Him in many ways and have driven Him from us. Now, if it seems right to you, let each one become reconciled to his brother, whom he has offended, and let brother graciously forgive brother. After we have humbled ourselves before God in this manner, let us march around Jerusalem in bare feet, and, with the aid of the relics of the Saints, invoke the mercy of the Lord, that the omnipotent God, who for us, His servants, assumed the flesh, who humbly rode into the city on an ass, to suffer death on the cross for our sins, may come to our aid. If we make this procession around the walls, for the honor and glory of His name, He will open the city to us and give us judgment upon His enemies and ours, who now contaminate the place where He suffered and the Holy Sepulcher; the enemy whom we, with the aid of divine humility and in order to obtain our own salvation, are trying to drive out." These words were pleasing to both princes and people, and it was publicly decided that on the next Friday the clergy should lead the procession with the crosses and the relics of the Saints, while the knights and all able-bodied men, with trumpets, standards, and arms, should follow them barefooted. All this we did according to the commands of God and the princes. When we reached that spot on the Mount of Olives, whence the Lord had ascended into Heaven after the Resurrection, the following exhortation was made to the people: "Now that we are on the very

The Capture of Jerusalem in 1099

spot from which the Lord made His ascension and we can do nothing more to purify ourselves, except that each one of us forgive his brother, whom he has injured, that the Lord may forgive us." What more? All were reconciled to each other, and with generous offerings we besought the mercy of God, that He should not now desert His people, whom He had led to such a glorious and splended goal. Thus the mercy of God was obtained and everything that had been against us was now favorable. But although we avoided many troubles in this way, one we could not escape. While we marched around the city in procession the Saracens and Turks made the circuit on the walls, ridiculing us in many ways. They placed many crosses on the walls in yokes [the yoke was put on a criminal's neck as a sign of disgrace], and made sport of them with blows and insulting actions. We, in turn, hoped to obtain the aid of God in storming the city by means of these same signs [the crosses], and we pressed the work day and night.

The duke of Normandy, the count of Flanders, and Gaston of Beert constructed machines, also mantlets.[1]

---

[1] These mantlets were used to shelter the men who were attacking. They were usually made of a wickerwork or basketwork of twigs and rods so as to be light enough to carry easily. They were generally covered with hides as a protection from the firebrands hurled down from the walls. Such shields could be held over the men who were working close to the wall, or could be used by men when making an assault. These mantlets seem to have been of great service to the crusaders at Jerusalem.

Parallel Source Problems in Medieval History

The direction of this work was assigned to Gaston by the princes, because he was a most noble lord, respected because of his skill and reputation, and he very cleverly hastened matters, by dividing the work.
5 The princes busied themselves with obtaining and bringing in the material, while Gaston supervised the work of construction.

Likewise count Raymond made William Richau superintendent of the work on Mount Zion, while the
10 bishop of Albara brought in the timber with Saracens and others. The count's men seized many Saracen castles and villages and forced the Saracens to work as though they were slaves. Thus fifty or sixty carried on their shoulders a great beam for the construc-
15 tion of machines at Jerusalem, that could not have been dragged by four pair of oxen. What more shall I say? All worked with a singleness of purpose, no one was slothful and no hands were idle. All worked without wages except the artisans, who were paid
20 from a collection taken from the people. However, the count [Raymond] paid his workmen from his own resources. Surely the hand of the Lord was with us and aided those who were working. When our efforts were ended and the machines completed,
25 the princes held a council and announced: "Let all prepare themselves for a battle on Thursday; in the mean time, pray, fast, and give alms. Hand over your animals and servants to the artisans and carpenters, that they may bring in beams, poles, stakes,

The Capture of Jerusalem in 1099

and branches to make mantlets. Every two knights should make one mantlet and one scaling ladder. Do not hesitate to work for the Lord, for our labors will soon be ended."

This proclamation was accepted by all. Then it was decided what part of the city each leader should attack and where his machines should be located. Meanwhile the Saracens in the city, noting the great number of machines that we had constructed, strengthened the weaker parts of the wall, so that it seemed that they could only be taken by the most desperate efforts. Because the Saracens had made so many and such strong fortifications to oppose our machines, the duke, the count of Flanders, and the count of Normandy spent the night before the day set for the attack, moving their machines, mantlets, and platforms to that side of the city which is between the church of St. Stephen and the valley of Jehosaphat. You who read this must not think that this was a light undertaking, for the machines were carried in parts, almost a mile to the place where they were to be set up. When morning came and the Saracens saw that all the machinery and tents had been moved during the night, they were amazed. Not only the Saracens were astonished, but our people as well, for they recognized that the hand of the Lord was with us. The change was made because the new point chosen for attack is more level, and thus suitable for moving the machines up to the walls, which cannot be done unless the ground is level, and thus it happened that the part of the city that seemed the weakest was not attacked because it was impossible to move the machines close to the walls. This part of the city is on the north.

The count [Raymond] and his men worked equally hard on Mount Zion, but they had much assistance from William Ebriacus and the Genoese sailors, who, although they had lost their ships at Joppa, as we have already related, had nevertheless been able to save ropes, mallets, spikes, axes, and hatchets, which were very necessary to us. But why delay the story? The appointed day arrived and the attack began. However, I want to say this first, that, according to our estimate and that of many others, there were sixty thousand fighting men within the city, not counting the women and those unable to bear arms, and there were not many of these. At the most we did not have more than twelve thousand able to bear arms, for there were many poor people and many sick. There were two or three hundred knights in our army as I reckon it, not more. I say this, that you may realize that nothing, whether great or small, which is undertaken in the name of the Lord can fail, as the following pages show.

Our men began to undermine the towers and walls. From every side stones were hurled from the tormenti [1] and the petrariæ and so many arrows that

[1] See note 2, p. 111.

The Capture of Jerusalem in 1099

they fell like hail. The servants of God were sustained by the premises of their faith for any result, whether they should be killed or would presently prevail over their enemies. The battle showed no indication of victory, but when the machines were drawn nearer to the walls they hurled not only stones and arrows, but also burning wood and straw. The wood was dipped in pitch, wax, and sulphur, then straw and tow were fastened on by an iron band, and when lighted, these firebrands were shot from the machines. All bound together by an iron band, I say, so that, wherever they fell, the whole mass held together and continued to burn. Such missiles, burning as they shot upward, could not be resisted by swords or by high walls; it was not even possible for the defenders to find safety down behind the walls. Thus the fight continued from the rising to the setting sun in such splendid fashion that it is difficult to believe that anything more glorious was ever done. Then we called on the Almighty God, our leader and guide, confident in His mercy. Night brought fear to both sides. The Saracens feared that we would take the city during the night or on the next day, for the outer works were broken through and the ditch was filled, so that it was possible to make an entrance through the wall very quickly. On our part, we feared only that the Saracens would set fire to the machines that were moved close to the walls, and thus improve their situation. Thus on both sides it was a night of watchfulness, labor, and sleepless caution. On one side, most certain hope; on the other, doubtful fear. We gladly labored to capture the city for the glory of God; they less willingly strove to resist our efforts for the sake of the laws of Mohammed. It is difficult to believe how great were the efforts made on both sides during the night.

When the morning came, our men eagerly rushed to the walls and dragged the machines forward, but the Saracens had constructed so many machines; that for each one of ours they now had nine or ten. Thus they greatly interfered with our efforts. This was the ninth day, on which the priest had said that we would capture the city [Peter Desiderius. See his prophesy, p. 123]. But what checked the fulfilment of the prophesy? Our machines were now shaken apart by the blows of many stones, and our men lagged because they were very weary. However, the mercy of the Lord remained, which is never overcome nor conquered, but always a source of support in times of adversity. One incident must not be omitted. Two women tried to bewitch one of the hurling machines, but a stone struck and crushed them as well as three slaves, so that their lives were extinguished and the evil incantations were averted.

By noon our men were greatly discouraged. They were weary and at the end of their resources.

The Capture of Jerusalem in 1099

There were many enemies resisting each one of ours; the walls were very high and strong, and the great resources and skill that the enemy exhibited in repairing their defenses seemed too great for us to overcome. But, while we hesitated, irresolute, and the enemy exulted in our discomfiture, the healing mercy of God inspired us and turned our sorrow into joy, for the Lord did not forsake us. While a council was being held to decide whether or not our machines should be withdrawn, for some were burned and the rest badly shaken to pieces, a knight on the Mount of Olives began to wave his shield to those who were with the count and others, signaling them to advance. Who this knight was we have been unable to find out.[1] At this signal our men again began to take heart, and some began to batter the wall, while others began to ascend by means of scaling ladders and ropes. Our archers shot burning firebrands, and in this way checked the attack that the Saracens were making upon the wooden towers of the duke and the two counts. These firebrands, moreover, were wrapped in cotton. This shower of fire drove the defenders from the walls. Then the duke quickly released the long drawbridge which had protected the side of the wooden tower next to the wall, and it swung down from the top, being fastened to the middle of the tower, making

---

[1] Note Raymond's desire to have his readers believe that this may have been a miracle.

a bridge, over which the men began to enter Jerusalem, bravely and fearlessly. Among those who entered first were Tancred and the duke of Lotharingia [Godfrey], and the amount of blood that they shed on that day is incredible. All ascended after them, and the Saracens now began to suffer.

Strange to relate, however, at this very time when the city was practically captured by the Franks, the Saracens were still fighting on the other side, where the count was attacking the wall, as though it should never be captured. But now that our men had possession of the walls and towers, wonderful sights were to be seen. Some of our men (and this was more merciful) cut off the heads of their enemies; others shot them with arrows, so that they fell from the towers; others tortured them longer by casting them into the flames. Piles of heads, hands, and feet were to be seen in the streets of the city. It was necessary to pick one's way over the bodies of men and horses. But these were small matters compared to what happened at the temple of Solomon, a place where religious services are ordinarily chanted. What happened there? If I tell the truth, it will exceed your powers of belief. So let it suffice to say this much at least, that in the temple and portico of Solomon, men rode in blood up to their knees and the bridle reins. Indeed, it was a just and splendid judgment of God, that this place should be filled with the blood of the unbelievers, when it had

The Capture of Jerusalem in 1099

suffered so long from their blasphemies. The city was filled with corpses and blood. Some of the enemy took refuge in the tower of David and petitioned count Raymond for protection, and surrendered the tower into his hands.

Now that the city was taken it was worth all our previous labors and hardships to see the devotion of the pilgrims at the Holy Sepulcher. How they rejoiced and exulted and sang the ninth chant to the Lord. It was the ninth day, the ninth joy and exultation, and of perpetual happiness. The ninth sermon, the ninth chant was demanded by all. This day, I say, will be famous in all future ages, for it turned our labors and sorrows into joy and exultation; this day, I say, marks the justification of all Christianity and the humiliation of paganism; our faith was renewed. "The Lord made this day, and we rejoiced and exulted in it," for on this day the Lord revealed Himself to His people and blessed them. On this day the lord Adhemar, bishop of Puy,[1] was seen in the city by many people. Many also testified that he was the first to scale the wall, and that he summoned the knights and people to follow him. . . . This day was the 15th of July.

[1] See note, p. 123.

PROBLEM IV

IV.—The Departure of the University from Paris

1229-1231

The Departure of the University from Paris

I. THE HISTORICAL SETTING OF THE PROBLEM[1]

THE universities were a direct outgrowth of the quickened intellectual activity that was a prominent characteristic of the general progress of the twelfth century. The only existing institutions of learning were the monastic and cathedral schools, which lacked the facilities needed to meet the new situation. The administrative organization that they possessed was capable of little more than a general supervision of the crowds of students that thronged to them as the only available educational centers. Before a permanent university could arise some new form of organization had to be worked out that could insure continuity as well as more solidarity and give cohesion to these large groups of students and teachers. Such a development was started at Paris during the last part of the twelfth century.

Famous teachers had made Paris a leading educational center. During the early part of the century the students had divided their allegiance between the monastic schools of St. Victor's or St. Genevieve and the cathedral school of Notre Dame, but by the last of the century the latter was left in control of the educational situation. However,

[1] For an account of the "dispersion" of 1229, or a general discussion of the University of Paris, see Vol. I of Rashdall, *Universities in the Middle Ages*, Oxford, 1895, 3 volumes.

the increasing numbers of students and teachers made regulation difficult for the authorities of the old school, who found themselves unable to do more than maintain some pretense of general oversight.

In the monasteries or the cathedrals teaching was placed in charge of a *scholasticus* or *chancellor*, who had the right to grant the license or permit to teach. As the number of teachers increased the masters began to demand some control over the admission of new men to their profession. The chancellor, who was not in sympathy with the teachers, showed favoritism or laxity, even conferring the license upon candidates whose chief qualification was a material bribe, while worthy men, having the support of the masters under whom they had studied, might be refused. In self defense the teachers began to unite in an association or guild which was soon able to get a certain measure of control over this situation. The young candidate for the license was forced to realize that his future depended more on compliance with the wishes of the masters than those of the chancellor. Thus a long struggle began between the chancellor, who was the survival of the old cathedral school, and the new association of masters. In this contest the masters perfected their organization and increased the authority and power of their association.

The chancellor and the bishop strove to suppress what was in reality a new school, which was fast becoming independent of the loose control of the old cathedral authority. It was a natural growth that could not be checked. In spite of his efforts to maintain his authority, the chancellor saw the different faculties of theology, canon law, medicine, and arts organize separately, but with arrangements for united action. This division was according to the educational ideas of the age, which re-

The Departure of the University from Paris

garded the arts course as preparatory to work in the three higher fields of knowledge.

As the arts had the greatest number of students, its faculty took a leading part in the struggle of the university for recognition. The students of Paris came from all parts of Europe, and quite naturally grouped themselves by racial alignment. Thus sometime in the early thirteenth century the faculty of arts separated into four divisions called nations—the French, the English, the Norman, and the Picard. Each of these nations chose a procurator as its head. An official called the rector was chosen as chief administrative officer for the whole college of arts. Just how far the organization into nations had progressed in 1229 it is impossible to say. There is no evidence to indicate the existence of a rector until somewhat later in the century.

As this association of masters began to realize its power it began to use the turbulent student body that it taught to aid in its fight for privileges and recognition. When any of the rights that it claimed were violated it literally went on a strike and suspended all teaching. Thus in 1200, as the result of a "town and gown" riot, the provost of the city of Paris made a raid on the student quarter by way of retaliation, killing several students. The masters used this situation to extort privileges from the king, Philip Augustus, who feared that the university would leave the city. The association of teachers began to formulate customs to regulate its own internal affairs, and its first written statutes probably date from 1210. The bishop and the chancellor tried to take this power away from the association. On one occasion the whole university was excommunicated, and all its regulations were declared to be illegal unless they had been sanctioned by the cathedral authorities. This was in vain, for even

Parallel Source Problems in Medieval History

earlier, in 1215, the papal legate had drawn up a set of statutes by which the university was given the right to make statutes for the regulation of its own affairs and to require an oath of obedience from its members, thereby gaining an important concession in its fight for independence.

The new association of masters thus found a valuable ally in the papacy. Some time between 1210 and 1216 Innocent III. had granted the association the right to choose a procurator to represent it at the papal court. His legate had embodied the privileges granted in various bulls in the statutes of 1215. The judicial powers of the chancellor over students were restricted, and in the matter of the license he was forbidden to exact oaths for the purpose of binding the candidates to himself. He was commanded to grant the license to such candidates as were presented by a majority of the masters in the higher faculties or by six masters of arts, three of whom were chosen by the faculty of arts.

Armed with privileges from kings and popes, the association was already a formidable institution in 1229. So great was the reputation of the university in western Europe that a threat of removal was a serious matter indeed. What made the riot of 1229 grow to such serious proportions was the hostility of the bishop and the papal legate, who were anxious to curb this refractory association that was becoming entirely too independent of all control. Thus they prejudiced the queen against the masters. Whether they thought that the university would not carry out its threat to leave Paris or whether they failed to realize the indignation that such removal would rouse, they were soon confronted by a storm of protest that even royalty was unable to resist. Agents of the university were active at Rome, and the pope made vigorous efforts to

The Departure of the University from Paris

adjust the trouble. Mere settlement of the original matter of dispute no longer satisfied the masters after they had withdrawn from Paris, and they insisted on new concessions. When the university returned, therefore, it had won a great victory, for the privileges that it had obtained from pope and royalty placed it in a new position that insured its independent development in the future.

II. THE AUTHORS OF THE ACCOUNTS

1. *Mathew of Paris*, author of the *Chronica Majora*, which contains the longest narrative account of the dispersion of 1229, was an Englishman by birth and sentiment. He was well informed, and also shows considerable independence of judgment in his writing. From 1189 to 1235 his *Chronica Majora* was copied from another chronicle, but the account of the dispersion of the University of Paris was an addition that is probably his own work. His surname, Paris, indicates some French connection, as does his knowledge of French places and the French language. It is possible that he may have studied at Paris, although there is no positive evidence of this fact. He shows much interest in the affairs of the university, and also because of a somewhat unfavorable attitude toward the French monarchy it must be remembered that his account is favorable to the university.

2. *William of Nangis* was a monk at the monastery of St. Denis in the latter part of the thirteenth century. The *Gesta Ludovici* (the *Deeds of Louis*) was written in the reign of Philip III., and was presented to the king by the author. William used other authors with great freedom, and his work is little more than a compilation. For the period between 1226 and 1248 he probably used the account of an author whose work is now lost, but we cannot

be sure how accurately he copied. His account should therefore be used with great caution. It is interesting more because of his attitude toward the event than for its reliability.

The other narrative accounts are very brief notices, but occasionally add new details, especially in regard to the places to which students and masters migrated. As these notices are inserted in chronicles along with other very different kinds of information, it is impossible to tell where or how the authors obtained their information about the dispersion of 1229.

3. *Alberic of Tres Fontes*, a Cistercian monk of Champagne, wrote from 1227 to 1251. His *Chronica* is therefore contemporary for the thirteenth century. His work was the product of immense reading, and is of considerable merit and value.

4. *Ralph of Coggeshall* was also a contemporary. He was a Cistercian monk, but little more is known about him. The *Chronicon Anglicanum* (*English Chronicle*) contains one or two interesting details regarding the dispersion.

5. The *Annales* of the English monastery of *Dunstable* extend from the year 1 to 1297. From 1201 it contains much useful information not found elsewhere.

6. The *Annales Stadenses*, by *Albert of Stade*, who lived from about 1200 to 1261, was begun in the year 1240. Thus his work is nearly contemporary, and it is probable that he had accurate information about the university.

7. The *Chronicon Fiscamense* (the *Chronicle of Fécamp*) is thought to have been written at Fécamp, although even this fact is not certain. It extends to 1253.

8. The *Mare Historiarum* was probably written by a *John of Columna*, who wrote about the middle of the thirteenth century.

The other extracts are of a different character from the

The Departure of the University from Paris

narrative accounts of the annals or chronicles. Thus in the charter granted by the French king we have a legal document from the royal chancellery drawn up in the regular form that was customary for such documents. Fixed rules were followed and the same forms observed, just as is true in the case of legal documents to-day. The same regularity of form was true of the papal letters, although the forms and style were different from the royal charter. It must be remembered that such documents contain far more accurate and reliable information than can be found in the chronicles.

Gregory IX. became pope March 19, 1227. He was probably a nephew of Innocent III. and, what is more important, studied at Paris and Bologna, so that he was familiar with the university and realized its importance. At the time of the trouble at Paris, Gregory was engaged in a struggle with Frederick II., whom he had excommunicated in 1227. On June 1, 1231, the pope was driven from the city of Rome by an uprising of the citizens. That the pope was able to give so much attention to the affairs of the university while he was engaged in such a struggle in Italy is a further indication of the importance he attached to the preservation of the university.

The original charter granted by Philip Augustus in 1200 and the statutes of Gregory for the university in 1231 have been translated by D. C. Munro, and may be found in the *Pennsylvania Translations and Reprints*, Volume II, No. 3.

III. QUESTIONS FOR STUDY

1. What was the immediate cause of the dispersion?
2. What other grievances did the university have, as shown by the letters of the pope?
3. What privileges had the masters and students obtained from the kings of France?

Parallel Source Problems in Medieval History

4. Where did the students go after they left Paris?
5. What weapons did the university use to defend itself and to gain new privileges?
6. What concessions did the university obtain in regard to the granting of the license?
7. What special privileges did the masters and students obtain in regard to trial and arrest?
8. Do the letters written by the pope in 1229 indicate that he had intentions of issuing a charter of liberties at that time?
9. What was the oath referred to by the pope in his letter of November 24, 1229?
10. What prohibitions were placed on the masters and students by the pope?
11. What means did the pope use to bring about a settlement of the trouble?
12. What can you say of the reputation of the university in western Europe?
13. What indications of an association of masters can you find in the translations? How would you describe the organization that existed at this time?
14. What specific guarantees did the university obtain that defined its relationship to the chancellor?
15. For what was the university really fighting?

IV. The Sources

1. *Mathew of Paris, Chronica Majora.*

In the same year [1229] on the second and third days before Cineres [Ash Wednesday], days on which the clerks [1] were accustomed to take a vacation, certain clerks went out from Paris to St. Marcel,[2] where there was fresh air and they could indulge in their usual sports. When they had enjoyed such recreation for some time, by chance they found there in a certain tavern good wine which was pleasant to drink. While there a quarrel arose between the drunken clerks and the inn keeper over the price of the wine and they began to give each other blows and to pull hair. Some of the men of the village rushed in to liberate the inn keepers, and, although the clerks fought back, they were compelled to flee, roundly beaten. Bruised and battered, they returned to the city, where they stirred up their companions to help them get revenge, and with their assistance on the next day they returned to St.

[1] The masters and students were regarded as clerks, and thus were entitled to the immunities and privileges of ecclesiastics.
[2] A suburb of Paris.

Marcel armed with swords and clubs. They violently entered the tavern, broke all the wine jars, and poured the wine on the floor. After this they went out on the streets and assaulted every one whom they met, whether man or woman, leaving them half dead from their blows.

The prior of St. Marcel, when he learned of the wrong that had been inflicted on his people, whom it was his duty to protect, went in person to the bishop of Paris and the Roman legate and registered a complaint. They in turn hastened to the queen, who was then in charge of the government, and asked her to punish such misdemeanors. With the impulsiveness of a woman and the haste of an agitated mind, she ordered the provost and the mercenary guard to arm quickly, go out from the city, and punish the perpetrators of this outrage, sparing none. These men, who were ready to carry out anything brutal, left the gates of the city armed, and found a large number of clerks engaged in sports outside the walls, but who had not been at all guilty of the above mentioned offense, for those who had started the trouble were from that region near Flanders which is commonly called Picardy. Notwithstanding this, the guards rushed upon the unarmed and innocent clerks without mercy, killing some, wounding others, and injuring others with blows. Some escaped by flight and concealed themselves in ditches or other hiding places. Among the

The Departure of the University from Paris

wounded, two clerks who were rich and prominent were found dead; one of them was a Fleming and the other belonged to the Norman people.

When the news of this violence reached the ears of the masters of the university, after first suspending all readings and disputations, they all went to the queen and legate and demanded that justice should be done immediately. It seemed unreasonable to them that for such small provocation—namely, the misdeeds of a few contemptible clerks — that the whole of them should suffer injury, for punishment ought rather to be administered to the person who had committed the offense. However, as justice was entirely denied them by the queen, the legate,[1] and the bishop of the city, there was a general migration of masters and students from the city. The teaching of the masters and the instruction of the students ceased, so that not one famous person of them all was left in the city. The city was deprived of its clerks, in whom it had been accustomed to glory. Among the famous Englishmen who left at this time were Master Alan of Beccles, Master Nicholas of Farnham, Master John Blund, Master Ralph of Maidenstone, Master William of Durham, and many others whom it would take too long to name. The departing clerks scattered themselves

---

[1] Cardinal Romain of St. Angelo was the papal legate at the time. In 1225 he had broken the university seal, and a mob of students and masters had attacked his house.

generally among the great cities of different countries. A great number of them, however, chose the metropolitan city of Angers for general instruction. . . . A certain clerk wrote an apostrophe—that is, as though a person were speaking—in which the city of Paris complains to the clerks.

"O clerks, I tremble with fear because you wish to scorn me.

"I am shaken with weeping; I mourn my loss; you flee from me."

Nevertheless, it was arranged through the agency of discrete persons that restitution should be made by both sides for their offenses, so that the clerks should have peace and the citizens were promised that the clerks would reform their ways and the whole of the students was recalled.

2. The *Gesta Ludovici* (the *Deeds of Louis*), by William of Nangis.

In the same year [1230] a great commotion arose at Paris, between the clerks and the citizens. The citizens killed some of the students, and on that account the clerks left Paris and scattered themselves among the different provinces of the world. When the king saw that the study of letters and philosophy would depart from Paris, those studies by which the treasures of knowledge are acquired, which precede and surpass all other treasures, and which had first come from Athens to Rome, and from Rome into France along with the glory of

The Departure of the University from Paris

chivalry, he began to be troubled. Fearing that such great and rich treasures would leave his kingdom, and as the riches of divine salvation are wisdom and knowledge, lest at some time God should say to him, "Because you have rejected knowledge I will reject you," the pious king commanded the clerks to return to Paris; and when they obeyed, he received them graciously, and quickly made the townsmen make reparation for everything that they had done to the clerks before. For if that most precious treasure, the knowledge of salvation, which formerly followed Dionysius the Areopagite[1] from Greece to Paris and the Gallic regions, along with faith and the renown of Chivalry, should be taken away from the kingdom of France, surely the banner of the king of France, decorated with the lily and on which the flower is painted with three leaves, would be disfigured in one of its parts.

3. *Chronica* of Alberic of Tres Fontes.

A most cruel and unfortunate struggle broke out at Paris at the beginning of Quadragesima, between the clerks and laymen over a matter of small importance. Those who tried to check it aroused by their actions the bitter hatred of the clerks, and the queen and lord cardinal himself were blamed. However, as many as were seized were punished.

---

[1] St. Denis was the first bishop of Paris and the patron saint of France. In popular legend he was identified with Dionysius the Areopagite, mentioned in Acts xvii, 34.

Parallel Source Problems in Medieval History

After much negotiation, as they were not able to arrange matters with complete satisfaction, only a few remained in the city, for all the others, including the most famous masters, departed. Many returned to their homes, while some died on the journey to Rome. Nevertheless, at the end of three years all the difficulties were settled, and those who wished to do so returned to Paris.

4. The *Chronicon Anglicanum* (the *English Chronicle*), by Ralph of Coggeshall.

At Paris a great discord arose between the citizens and the students of the city, and a great many noble clerks as well as poor clerks were killed, while nearly twenty were thrown into the Seine. Certain of the masters went to the lord pope, complaining of such persecution, while others with their students migrated to other cities. The city was prohibited to students, and was emptied of both students and teachers, although up to this time it was more famous and distinguished than all other cities, because of the excellent teachers in the different schools.

5. The *Annales of Dunstable*.

In the same year the whole body of the masters and students of Paris was moved to the city of Angers. Only a few teachers remained at Paris, and these were notable neither in number nor reputation.

6. The *Annales Stadenses* (the *Annals of Stade*).

A great uprising occurred at Paris between the

The Departure of the University from Paris

clerks and the people, and many clerks were killed. On this account the University was removed to Angers.

7. The *Chronicon Fiscamense* (the *Chronicle of Fécamp*).

A discord arose between the queen and the clerks of Paris, and many were drowned in the Seine.

8. The *Mare Historiarum*.

In the above mentioned year [1230] a riot broke out between the students and citizens of Paris, and proceeded in such a way that for a time the university and that wonderful multitude, which had gathered from every region under heaven, departed. Some of them went to Rheims, some to Angers, some to Orleans, some to England, and others into Lombardy to Bologna.

9. *Order of the Provisors, closing the University* (March 27, 1229).

In the name of the Father, Son, and Holy Ghost, we, the appointed provisors of the whole body, by common consent and agreement do order and command that, unless satisfactory reparation is made to the whole body of masters and students for the atrocious injuries suffered by them from the Provost of Paris, his accomplices and certain others, within one month after Easter day, no one shall be permitted to remain in the city or diocese of Paris to study, either for the purpose of teaching or being taught. For a period of six years, beginning at the end of the aforesaid month, no one shall teach either publicly or privately. Nor shall any one be permitted to return at the end of the six years unless satisfactory reparation is made for the aforesaid injuries. And to make this binding, we jointly attach to this charter our seals.

Dated the twelve hundred and twenty-eighth year of our Lord, in the month of March, on the day after the Annunciation of the Lord.

10. *Letter of Henry III. of England to the Masters and Students of Paris* (July 16, 1229).

The king, to the Masters and the Body of Students at Paris, Greeting.

We piously hope for the betterment of your condition and that it will be changed to one of deserved freedom, for you have suffered with fitting humility the trials and tribulations that you have been forced to endure under the iniquitous law of Paris, and through it all you have shown due reverence to God and the Holy Church. Hence, we announce to the whole of you that if it should please you to transfer yourselves to our kingdom of England and remain in it for the purpose of study that we will assign to you whatever boroughs, cities, or villages that you may select. Further, we will see to it that you shall enjoy every possible liberty and assurance of peace that is pleasing to God and would completely satisfy you.

Witnessed by the king at Reading, the sixteenth day of July.

The Departure of the University from Paris

11. *Confirmation of the Privilege Issued by Philip Augustus in 1200,[1] by Louis IX.* (August, 1229; Fontainebleau).

In the name of the holy and undivided Trinity, Amen. Louis, by the grace of God, King of the Franks. Be it known to all persons, present and future, that we have found the charter granted by our famous grandfather, Philip, formerly illustrious king of the Franks, and it reads as follows:

"In the name of the holy and undivided Trinity, Amen. Philip, by the grace of God, King of the Franks. Be it known to all persons, present and future, that, because of that disgraceful riot in which five of the clerks and laymen of Paris were killed by certain malefactors, we will give justice as follows: Concerning that Th. [omas], who was provost at the time and concerning whom above all others the clerks have made complaint, we promise to keep him in chains forever because he denies the deed, and he shall remain a prisoner in the citadel on poor food as long as he lives, unless he shall decide to take the ordeal of water publicly in Paris. If he fails in this he will be condemned; if he proves his innocence he will never again be our provost or our bailiff either in Paris or elsewhere in our land as long as we are able to prevent it in justice, and, furthermore, he will never be allowed to enter the city of

[1] This was the Charter of Liberties issued by Philip Augustus in 1200.

Paris. If by good and legal inquest, which we have committed to two of our faithful subjects, G. [alterus] the Chancellor and Ph. [illip] of Levis, which shall be conducted without consideration of persons and under oath in the faith by which they are Christians and that which they owe to us, their liege lord, also under oath which they shall make to us concerning our honor and counsel, we can discover what we are able and ought to do, that we will do without delay, saving the honor of God and of ourselves. Concerning the others who are in prison for the same offense, we will do this, to wit: we will keep them in perpetual confinement unless they purge themselves by the ordeal of water, with God as witness. If they fail in this we will consider them condemned, unless any of them shall be freed from prison by us because of a good inquest by the students. Concerning those who have fled, we hold them condemned by reason of their flight, and we will have all the provosts in our land swear that they will seek them diligently, and if they are able to seize any one of them they shall arrest him and send him to us at Paris.

"Moreover, concerning the security of the scholarly clerks of Paris, with the counsel of our men we have ordained as follows for the future: that we will make all citizens of Paris swear that if any one shall witness an injury done to a student by a layman, he shall give truthful testimony concerning the affair, neither

The Departure of the University from Paris

shall any one go away so that he may not see. And if it should happen that any one should witness an injury done to a student by a layman and if the student is struck by arms, or a club, or a stone, all
5 laymen who witness the act in good faith shall seize that malefactor or malefactors and hand him over to our justice, nor shall they run away so that they will not be able to make seizure or to give truthful testimony. Moreover, whether the malefactor shall
10 be arrested for this offense or not, we will make legal inquest, either by clerks or laymen or any persons whatsoever, and our provost and justices shall do the same. If we are able to discover by legal inquest, or our justices are able to discover that the accused
15 committed that offense, we will immediately give justice, or our justice will do the same, according to the nature of the offense, even though the malefactor should deny the offense or say that he is prepared to defend himself by single combat or to prove his
20 innocence by the ordeal of water.

"Moreover, henceforth our provost or our justices shall not be permitted to lay hands on a student or to put him in our prison unless it is clear that the offense of the student is one for which he
25 ought to be arrested, and then our justice will arrest him on the spot without any violence, unless he should resist, and hand him over to ecclesiastical justices, who ought to keep him in custody both for our satisfaction and that of the person injured.

Parallel Source Problems in Medieval History

If the offense should appear serious our justice shall be sent, so that he may find out what should be done with the student. If, however, the student arrested should not resist and should confess the offense, according to the findings of the inquest mentioned above and the aforesaid oath, we will administer suitable punishment. Furthermore, our justice shall not seize the chief of the students of Paris for any offense, but if it is evident that they should be seized it should be done according to ecclesiastical justice, so that they shall be kept in custody and the chattels shall be dealt with as they would be if they had been legally confiscated by the Church. However, if students are arrested by our provost at such an hour that an ecclesiastical justice cannot be found or found quickly, then our provost shall have them put under guard in any student house until they can be handed over to ecclesiastical justices, but without violence, as we have said above.

"In regard to the lay servants of the scholarly clerks who do not owe us *burgensium* or *residentium* [1] and do not live by trade in order that the students may not be able to do injury to others by means of such servants it shall be as follows: we will not lay

---

[1] *Burgensium* or Burgage was the fixed tax that the citizen of a town paid to the lord or king. *Residentium* was the right of a feudal lord to compel his vassal or tenant to live within the limits of his fief.

The Departure of the University from Paris

hands on them, nor will our justice, unless the offense is apparent and one for which our justice ought to make arrest. However, notwithstanding what the contents of this privilege, which we grant to the students of Paris, may be, we do not intend to include the canons of Paris and their servants in this privilege, but we wish that the servants of the canons of Paris and the canons of the same town should have the same liberties that our predecessors have been accustomed to allow them. Concerning any difficulty that might arise from any of the aforesaid arrangements, or concerning this charter, we cannot be brought to trial except in our own court.

"That this charter may be more carefully preserved and shall be more binding by law forever, we decree that our provost and the people of Paris, in the presence of the students, shall swear that they will observe the terms mentioned above in good faith. Further, whoever shall in the future be given the office of Provost by us shall, at the very beginning of his provostship—namely, on the first or second Sunday—take oath publicly, in the presence of the students, that he will observe everything above mentioned in good faith."

We [Louis] approve and command everything said above, and we command that it be confirmed by the authority of our royal seal and by the stamp of our signature below.

Parallel Source Problems in Medieval History

Dated at Fontainebleau in the twelve hundred and twenty-ninth year of our Lord, in the month of August, in the third year of our reign, with those present in our palace whose names are signed below. No Seneschall present. (Signed) Robert, Butler. (Signed) Bartholomew, Chancellor. (Signed) Mathew, Constable.[1]

12. *Letter of Gregory IX. to William, Bishop of Paris* (November 23, 1229).

... To the Bishop of Paris.

Believing that we had found a man after our own heart and that we could rightly rejoice and exult in you, we poured the oil upon your head with sacred unction, so that by retaining in yourself the grace of religion, you would give to those about you the odor of good reputation. We thought that, having chosen you with care, you would perform the duties of your office in such a manner that you would deservedly hear from the highest *Paterfamilias*, "Well done, good and faithful servant; enter thou into the glories of the Lord," because you would have offered him double the talents that he had intrusted to your keeping. We, moved by reports that we had heard about you rather than by any personal knowledge of you, placed you above others who were known and tried, when we intrusted the church of Paris to your keeping, and this cannot be concealed, for it

---

[1] The original document has a fragment of wax seal attached by a green silk cord.

The Departure of the University from Paris

is like a city placed upon a mount. Moreover, we boasted that we had made Sabaoth a useful cultivator in the garden of the Lord. But lo, grieving, we return, bearing a wound from an unexpected enemy, our hope disappointed, for we are so confounded by your acts that we are forced to say, although unwillingly, "We regret that we made this man." . . .

We know, a dissension having arisen between our most dear son in Christ [Louis], the king of the Franks, and [Blanche] the queen, his mother, both illustrious, on the one side, and our beloved sons, the masters and students of Paris, on the other side, that these same masters, with their students, were so exasperated by the injuries and grievances that they suffered, that they have departed from Paris and have removed the university elsewhere. You not only have not tried to be a mediator in this affair, but it is said that you have actually given such counsel and advice as would prevent the agreements proposed by either side from being accepted. Hoping to produce such benefits as would come if the university was recalled, and desiring to have the inconveniences that have resulted from its departure removed, we are commanding in our letters to our brothers [Maurice] of Le Mans and [Guarinus] of Senlis, bishops, and to our dear son, master John, archdeacon of Chalons, that they should act as mediators between the king and queen and the

Parallel Source Problems in Medieval History

masters and students, and should use diligent solicitude and make effective efforts in order that the restoration of the privilege granted by Ph. [ilip], king of the Franks, of illustrious memory, should
⁵ satisfy the aforesaid masters and students for the injuries and sufferings that they have endured and thus the university of Paris may be recalled. . . .

As a brother, we ask you and exhort in the Lord
¹⁰ by apostolic letter, and command you by strict admonishment, that you bestir yourself carefully but effectively, and prudently persist in so doing until suitable satisfaction shall be made to the masters and students aforesaid for the injuries that they have
¹⁵ endured and thus the university may be recalled to Paris, and that the substantial privilege be restored to them so that these studies shall be preserved. Thus, you may atone for the stain of your former offense or negligence, and we shall be less put to shame
²⁰ through you, for we cannot pass these matters by with closed eyes. In some other way we will provide a way, the Lord helping, for the correction of what is not so much your negligence as deliberate wilfulness on your part. In this way you may be
²⁵ able to recognize, through penance, how much you have sinned.

Dated at Perugia, the ninth day before the Calends of December, in the third year of our pontificate.

The Departure of the University from Paris

13. *Letter of Gregory IX. to the bishops of Le Mans and Senlis and the Archdeacon of Chalons* (November 24, 1229).

To [Maurice] of Le Mans and [Guarinus] of Senlis, Bishops, and Master John, Archdeacon of Chalons.

Know that it has reached our ears that a dissension has arisen between our most dear son [Louis], the king of France, and [Blanche] his mother, the queen, both illustrious, on the one side, and our beloved sons, the masters and students of Paris, on the other side, and that these same masters with their students were so exasperated by the injuries and grievances which they suffered that they have departed from Paris, and have removed the university elsewhere, and by so doing they seem to have carried the key of knowledge with them and to wish to close the kingdom of Heaven for mankind, inasmuch as they themselves are unwilling to enter, and they seem to be unwilling to let others enter who desire to do so. Hoping to produce such benefits as would come from the return of the aforesaid river to its channel, and desiring to overcome the inconveniences that have resulted from its departure, we command, by apostolic letter, that you should carefully act as mediators between the king and queen and the masters and students aforesaid, and that you use diligent solicitude and make effective efforts, in order that the restoration of the privilege granted by

Parallel Source Problems in Medieval History

Ph. [ilip], king of the Franks, of illustrious memory, should satisfy the masters and students aforesaid for the sufferings and injuries that they have endured, and thus the university of Paris may be recalled.

The force of that other oath should not be permitted to interfere, for of the three principles that it required, two seem to have been lacking—namely, justice and judgment—and, having originated thus, it would seem that such an oath ought not to have much force. If perchance some people should try to excuse themselves by such difficulties, with the aid of the Lord and the foresight of the Apostolic See, we will endeavor to arrange matters, so that they will not be spotted by the stain of any sin of this kind. And since delay seems to increase the dangers in this matter, we command that whatever can be done without delay shall be done, and that you inform us whatever you learn about these matters as soon as possible, so that when we are instructed by your report, we may proceed in this matter, the Lord helping.

Dated at Perugia, on the eighth day before the Calends of December, in the third year.

14. *Letter of Gregory IX. to Louis, King of France, and Blanche, his Mother* (November 26, 1229).

To [Louis] King of the Franks, and [Blanche] the Queen, his Mother, Both Illustrious.

Know that it has come to our ears that a dissen-

The Departure of the University from Paris

sion has arisen between you, on the one side, and our beloved sons, the masters and students of Paris, on the other side, that these same masters with their students were so exasperated by the injuries and grievances which they suffered that they have departed from Paris and have removed the university elsewhere. Hoping to produce such benefits as would come if the university were recalled, and desiring to have the inconveniences that have resulted from its departure removed, we are commanding in our letters to our venerable brothers [Maurice] of Le Mans and [Guarinus] of Senlis, bishops, and to Master John, archdeacon of Chalons, that as our representatives they should act as mediators between you and the masters and students aforesaid, and should use diligent solicitude and make effective efforts in order that the restoration of the privilege granted by Ph. [ilip], king of the Franks, of illustrious memory, should satisfy the aforesaid masters and students for the injuries and sufferings that they have endured, and thus the university of Paris should be recalled. Therefore, we ask your excellency, and advise and exhort in the Lord, and in adherence to the blessed benignity of your predecessors, as well as the reverence that you have toward the Apostolic See and toward us, that you admit these men into your royal grace and favor; that you acquiesce in the advice and exhortation of these aforesaid men and be prompt in the settle-

ment of this affair, just as you will be if you follow
your usual clemency. Lest, if you do otherwise,
which we do not believe will be the case, we should
see wisdom and benignity, without which the unity
of power is scarcely able to exist, cast aside, and we,
who are not able to permit this kingdom [of France],
which has thus far been blessed by Heaven, to be
dishonored in any such manner, would be forced to
make other arrangements in this matter.

Dated at Perugia, the sixth day before the Calends
of December, in the third year of our pontificate.

15. *Letter of Gregory IX. to the Masters and Students
at Paris and Angers* (May 10, 1230).

To the masters and students sojourning at Paris
and Angers.

. . . Because the ancient enemy of the human race
and the diabolical destroyer of peace recently strove
to diminish the increase of happiness by his cunning, and, though it grieves me to say it, has succeeded in diminishing it, for a dissension has arisen
between you and the citizens of Paris, the study
of theological learning and the principles of
scholastic training have ceased in the aforesaid
city. We, who cherish the honor of the same city,
and are not able and ought not to permit a decline
in such studies, desire to bring about their reformation, lest, if they should be further removed, they
should be completely destroyed. Although we have
seen certain plans and plenty of other petitions,

The Departure of the University from Paris

we are not able to obtain sufficient knowledge concerning the matter in hand, because we are not able to proceed without you, whom the business especially concerns. Thus, by our authority, we command your presence, and we hereby issue strict injunctions that you will send to us at the feast of the Blessed Virgin, certain persons, who shall be qualified to represent the whole body of you. Because of this, we have arranged for the detention of Master W.[1] Further, in order that we may be fully informed of your liberties, and that we may expedite matters more surely, we wish and command that you send to us, under authentic seals, copies of all privileges and indulgences that you have received from us or from kings.

Dated at the Lateran, on the sixth day before the Ides of May, in the fourth year of our pontificate.

16. *Letter of Gregory IX. to the Masters and Students of Paris* (February 27, 1231). The Bull called *Parens Scientiarum.*

Gregory, Bishop, Servant of the Servants of God, to his dear Sons, all the Masters and Students of Paris. Greeting and Apostolic Blessing. . . .

Since it is not doubtful that it would greatly displease both God and men, if any one should try to disturb such distinguished excellence as is found

---

[1] William of Auxerre, author of important theological works, appears to have been sent to Rome by the king with letters to the pope.

in the aforesaid city [Paris], or who should forcefully and mightily oppose with all his strength any one which might disturb such a condition of affairs, we have listened diligently to the complaints that have been presented to us and decided the matter, aided by the advice of our brothers, rather by precautionary measures than with judicial judgment, concerning the trouble that has arisen in that city owing to diabolical instigation and which has so greatly disturbed the university. As to the status of the students and the schools, we have decreed that the following regulations must be observed, to wit: that whoever shall next be created chancellor of Paris must be elected in the presence of the bishop or at his command, in the chapter of Paris, and two masters shall be summoned and present on this occasion representing the whole body of students. At his installation he shall take oath that, for the regulation of theology and decretals [canon law], in good faith and according to his conscience at every time and place, with due consideration for the welfare of the city and the honor and reputation of its faculties, he will not confer the license unless it is deserved, and will not admit unworthy persons when the approval of persons and nations is lacking. Indeed, before he shall license any one within a period of three months from the time when petition is made for the license, he shall diligently make inquiry from all masters of theology in the city as well as from

The Departure of the University from Paris

other upright and learned men, from whom the truth can be obtained, concerning the morality, learning, eloquence, probable future, and all other matters which are required on such occasions; and when he has made such inquiry, in good faith, according to what is right and expedient, and according to the dictates of his conscience, he shall grant or refuse the license to the candidate seeking it. Moreover, the masters of theology and decretals, when they begin to teach, shall take public oath that they will give faithful testimony regarding the matters previously considered. The chancellor shall likewise take oath that he will in no way reveal the advice of the masters to their prejudice, but that he will do all in his power to preserve the regulations of Paris, openly and legally (as they were in the beginning). Concerning the students of medicine, of the arts and others, the chancellor shall promise to examine the masters in good faith, and that he will not admit any who are not worthy, but will refuse the unworthy. Further, inasmuch as confusion creeps in wherever there is disorder, we grant to you the right to make prudent regulations and ordinances concerning the manner and hours of readings and discussions,[1] concerning the prescribed

---

[1] Teaching consisted of readings and discussions. The reading was the elucidation of an old author by the teacher, hence the term for teaching was "to read." The masters or the students held frequent discussions, or debates, in which they tested their

dress,[1] the burial of the dead, concerning the hours at which bachelors may teach and what they ought to teach,[2] likewise concerning the rent and prohibition of hospices,[3] and further grant to you the right to punish all who refuse to obey such regulations and ordinances, by expulsion from the society. If, perchance, the rating of hospices is removed from your control, or because it is not in your control, any of your people should suffer injury or wrong— namely, death or mutilation of body—unless, after due warning has been given in advance, reparation is made within fifteen days, you shall have the right to suspend teaching until satisfaction is obtained. Further, if any of your people happen to be imprisoned without just cause, if the molestation does not cease after warning has been given, you have the

learning and their skill in logic or dialectics. Ordinary readings or lectures were those which were regular and had precedence over the extraordinary, which could not be given until the ordinary readings were finished.

[1] "No master lecturing in arts should have a cloak unless it is round and black and reaching to the heels at least when it is new. He may well wear the pallium [garment worn by monks]. He is not to wear under the round cloak embroidered shoes, and never any with long bands."—*Statutes of 1215*.

[2] After the student had completed a certain amount of work and had been in residence a stated period, he took an examination which made him a bachelor. The bachelor continued to pursue studies under masters, but was also required to do some teaching.

[3] The hospice was a house in which students lived. A senior student, or a bachelor, was chosen to act as steward, or general manager. With the influx of students the rents of houses in the student quarter had become excessive. See the letter of Gregory to Louis, No. 18, p. 173.

The Departure of the University from Paris

right to immediately suspend all teaching, if you believe that by so doing you can help matters.

We command, further, that the bishop of Paris should thus correct excessive delinquency, that the honor of the students should be preserved, and that wrongdoing should not go unpunished, but, in any case of delinquency, innocent persons must not be arrested. If, however, a probable suspicion shall have arisen against any one, with fitting caution and in an honorable manner, he should be taken into custody, but he shall be spared all the exacting delays of imprisonment. If, perchance, he has committed a crime that demands imprisonment, the bishop shall detain the guilty party in his prison, for the chancellor is absolutely forbidden to have a prison of his own. Further, we prohibit the seizure of students for debts contracted by another, since this is prohibited by canonical and legal decrees. Neither the bishop, nor any of his officers, nor the chancellor shall exact a money penance for the removal of the decree of excommunication or any other censure, nor shall the chancellor extort from masters about to be licensed any oath or promise of obedience, nor shall he receive any other consideration or promise for granting the license, but shall be content with the oath above described.

Hereafter, summer vacations shall not last more than a month, but, if they so wish, bachelors may teach during vacations. We expressly forbid students to roam about the town with arms, and the whole body of you should not defend those who disturb the peace or the university. Those who pretend that they are students but do not frequent the schools or are not attached to any master shall not enjoy the privileges of students. We command, further, that masters of arts should give one course in Priscian,[1] and should always give one other ordinary.[2] Those books of natural philosophy which were prohibited by the provincial council for a definite cause,[3] shall not be used at Paris until they have been examined and purged of every suggestion of error. The masters and students of theology should strive to occupy themselves in a laudable manner in the field which they profess, and should not try to be philosophers, but should rather seek to become learned about God. They should not speak in the language of the people, and confuse the sacred language with the profane, but should discuss such questions in the schools as can be definitely settled by the theological books or the treatises of the holy fathers.

In regard to the property of students who die

[1] Priscian was the author of the grammar that was used in the universities of the Middle Ages.

[2] Ordinary course of reading which was given at the regular hours of the regular term.

[3] The provincial council of Paris to which Gregory refers was that of 1210. The works of Aristotle on natural philosophy were condemned at this time, while the statutes of 1215 forbid the use of Aristotle's natural philosophy and his metaphysics.

The Departure of the University from Paris

intestate or who have not committed the settlement of their affairs to others, we have decided that the bishop and one of the masters, chosen for this purpose by the whole body, shall collect all the goods of the deceased in a safe place, and when they have made such arrangement they shall fix a date by which it shall be possible to send the news of such death to the home of the deceased, and those upon whom the succession to such goods falls shall be able to come to Paris or send a satisfactory representative, and if they should come or should send, the goods should be handed over to them with suitable caution. If no one should appear, then the master and the bishop should leave the property as a bequest for the soul of the deceased according to their judgment, unless the heirs have some good reason for not coming, in which case the disposal of the property shall be deferred.

Indeed, because the masters and students, irritated by wrongs and injuries, have bound themselves by oath and have departed from the city of Paris, thus breaking up the university, and they seem to have made it not so much an individual matter as a common affair, we, in the interest of the general Church and its well considered advantage, enjoin and command that when privileges shall have been granted to masters and students, by our dear son in Christ [Louis]—king of the Franks—and the punishment of the malefactors who injured them has been determined, they should see to it at Paris that nothing of censure should be brought forth concerning their absence or return or irregularity. No man whatsoever shall be permitted to infringe or to oppose without grave risk to himself, this our charter of provisions, constitutions, concessions, prohibitions, and inhibitions. If, moreover, any one should presume to try this he should know that he will incur the displeasure of the Almighty God and of Peter and Paul, His blessed apostles.

Dated at the Lateran, on the Ides of April, in the fifth year of our pontificate.

17. *Letter of Gregory IX. to Odo, Abbot of Saint Germain-des-Près* (April 13, 1231).

Gregory, Bishop, Servant of the Servants of God, to his dear son [Odo], Abbot of Saint Germain-des-Près, Paris, Greeting and Apostolic Blessing.

Inasmuch as students ought to be not in worse but in better relations to you and your men than to other citizens of the city of Paris, we advise you by apostolic letter to be discreet, and in advising we command you to bind your men in the village of St. Germain by the same restrictions as those by which the citizens of Paris are bound by royal privilege for the peace and security of the students. Fulfil this our request in such a way that you will show yourself friendly and agreeable to these same students, not so much because of necessity as by your

The Departure of the University from Paris

own free will, and you will render yourself most deserving both of divine grace and of ours.

Dated at the Lateran, on the Ides of April, in the fifth year of our pontificate.

18. *Letter of Gregory IX. to Louis, King of France* (April 18, 1231).

Gregory, Bishop, Servant of the Servants of God, to our most dear son in Christ [Louis], King of the Franks, Greeting and Apostolic Blessing.

Just as it is to the interest of the kingdom of heaven that the university should be established in that city in its former position, so it will benefit your honor and safety to carry out with obliging grace and zeal the arrangements that have been made by us. Wherefore, we ask your serenity, and advise and exhort in the Lord, that you follow the example of your ancestors and show yourself favorable and benign to the students, and that you renew and observe and force others to observe the privilege granted to them by King Philip, of glorious memory, your grandfather. Inasmuch as many are compelled to take hospices that are much too dear, grant to them further, without hesitation, that the regulation of hospices shall be placed in the hands of two masters and two citizens, who shall faithfully give oath and shall be chosen for this purpose with the consent of the masters; or, if the citizens are not interested in the matter, it shall be done by two masters, as has formerly been the custom.[1] And since it is to your honor as a king that you should carefully give justice for all injuries, see to it that the reparation that is said to have been arranged for the injuries that the students recently suffered shall be fulfilled. So fulfil our prayers and admonishments that you shall be worthy of divine favor and we shall be able to commend deservedly your clemency.

Dated at the Lateran, on the eighteenth day before the Calends of May, in the fifth year of our pontificate.

[1] See note, p. 168.

PROBLEM V

V.—The Coronation of Cola di Rienzo

The Coronation of Cola di Rienzo

I. THE HISTORICAL SETTING OF THE PROBLEM

THE career of Cola di Rienzo or Nicholas, son of Lawrence, reached its height with his coronation as tribune of the people in the first half of the month of August, 1347. Three months before that time he had been a poor peasant who gloried in the office of papal notary at Rome; four months later he was a fugitive from the wrath of the pope. Meantime he had been ruler of Rome, almost worshiped by the people of the city, honored by neighboring states, and applauded by kings and even by the pope. The circumstances which made possible this spectacular rise of a mere peasant to the dizzy height of imperial ambition involve most of the forces which were operating in early Renaissance Italy, and especially at Rome.

Rome itself had for almost half a century been the scene of unusual turbulence. The papal curia, which had been one of her greatest sources of wealth as well as importance, had been moved to Avignon in 1308. In that same year a devastating fire had swept over a great part of the city, adding greatly to the already overstocked supply of ruins. In 1312 the emperor Henry VII. made his chimerical journey to receive the imperial crown, and had to fight his way through the city to the Capitol. Ludwig of Bavaria, who came to Italy for a similar purpose

Parallel Source Problems in Medieval History

sixteen years later, had to wage war on Roman soil also. At the other times the city was largely at the mercy of certain noble families whose intense rivalry kept it in almost constant turmoil. These families, of which the Colonna, the Orsini, the Gætani, and the Frangipani were the leading ones, had, even in the days when the popes were at Rome, been powerful enough to be troublesome. Now they fairly reveled in civil warfare. Their homes in the city were heavily barricaded and further fortified by bands of hired ruffians drawn from the streets of the city or from bands of roving free-booters. With these forces they rode about preying upon commerce and industry and terrifying the neighborhood. The common people had to choose one or another of these families as their patrons, and, whichever they chose, they became immediately legitimate prey for the others. Robbery was a genteel occupation, murder a daily occurrence, while respectable family life among the ordinary citizens became almost impossible. Occasionally the people had revolted and established popular governments based on the guild organization, but without permanent success. The powerful king of Naples, who had frequently interfered in the interests of the papacy, died in 1343, and the beautiful but wicked Joanna, who followed him, caused such anarchy that Naples could then be of little assistance.

The papacy, though at Avignon, was especially concerned about the condition of Rome. Rome and the papal states constituted the patrimony of St. Peter—a source of revenue and, in theory, of temporal independence. Over it the popes placed their officials, both spiritual and lay, and from it they drew feudal dues. As long as Robert of Naples was alive the popes were generally able to maintain order, but with his death there seemed

The Coronation of Cola di Rienzo

no effective means of controlling the lands. Ludwig of Bavaria, who had been elected emperor, was excommunicate, and Charles of Bohemia was chosen in his place in 1346. Neither was in a position to aid the papacy. The noble families were too strongly rivals to establish peace, while the adventurous free-booters who roamed about with powerful bands could scarcely be expected to look after the interests of the popes. Rienzo's success, therefore, was hailed with joy by the papacy at first, as well as by the people of the city.

Cola di Rienzo was the son of a poor tavern keeper in Rome, where he was born about the year 1314. Although his parents were poor, he seems, nevertheless, to have procured some education. His biographer accords him the reputation of being better versed in classical writings, and especially in deciphering inscriptions, than any other Roman of his time. He seems also to have had a natural gift for oratory, the effect of which was greatly enhanced by his fine appearance. Along with this he had an almost mystic imagination to which the things about him appeared in a strange light. Even in his early life many things had happened which afforded choice food for such a mind. Henry VII. had made his journey to re-establish the Roman Empire in 1312, and left a vivid impression upon the minds of the people. Dante's *De Monarchia* and his other writings laudatory of the old empire strengthened and prolonged that idea. When Rienzo was fourteen years old Ludwig of Bavaria came to Rome and had himself made emperor by the Roman people, supported by the writings of the theorist, Marsigilio of Padua, whose writings were quite widely read. Then in 1341 Rienzo witnessed the coronation of Petrarch, who had come to Rome to receive the laurel wreath where Cicero and Virgil had lived. The Rome of his imagination became, therefore, constantly more vivid and attainable.

His own Rome, as it was, served to his mind only as a violent contrast to what it ought to be. His own younger brother had been ruthlessly murdered by some of the noble faction, which could only embitter the grief he already felt for the sad plight of the city. In the popular overthrow of the government at the end of the year 1342 Rienzo was selected as orator to inform the pope and make the usual request for the return of the papacy to Rome. At Avignon he created a very favorable impression, and, though Clement VI. treated the question of return to Rome with the same indifference as his immediate predecessors, he did grant the not altogether altruistic plea for another jubilee at Rome in 1350. There, too, Rienzo met and became acquainted with Petrarch, and just before he left Avignon he received from the pope the office of papal notary in Rome. When he came home he found himself a man of more importance than the new office which he had would ordinarily confer.

In this office, however, he came into closer contact with the leading men in Rome; he learned more intimately the sordid side of the relations between the nobles, and he accumulated a fund of practical experience which he later utilized. Though he seems to have done little that was unusual during this period before his sudden rise in 1347, even that little was in the direction of his later work. Rome was startled by the appearance in a public place of an allegorical representation of Rome tossed about on a stormy sea among shipwrecks. This was ascribed to him. Later he discovered the tablet of the Lex Regia, which commemorated the grant of the imperium by the Senate to Vespasian. This was installed prominently in a public place; around it was painted the scene of the Senate

The Coronation of Cola di Rienzo

conferring the empire, and then Rienzo, dressed in fantastic garb, mounted a tribune and expounded the meaning of this tablet in a lecture more political than antiquarian. The nobles did not regard him as seriously then as they did later, but the people seem to have been duly impressed. Then a secret conspiracy was formed in which Rienzo and the papal vicar, Raymond of Orvieto, were the leaders. Plans were carefully laid; and on the 20th of May, when most of the Colonna forces were out of the city, the people were called together; Rienzo read a new constitution to them, and he with the papal vicar were made tribunes of the Roman people.

It has been generally admitted that the new government accomplished wonders. The nobles were suppressed; Rome and its neighborhood were peaceful; the city was effectively policed; fields that lay idle through fear were again cultivated, and pilgrims could come without fear of hurt to the holy shrines at Rome. The news of these events brought great rejoicing everywhere, and letters and presents poured into Rome from all Europe. Sailors said that even the Sultan of Babylon trembled at the very mention of the tribune's name. At any rate, Europe was pleased, and Cola felt immeasurably flattered and immoderately great.

John of Vico, the prefect of the city, was the last powerful opponent in the vicinity, but by the 16th of July even he was forced to prostrate himself at the feet of the tribune. On the 26th of that month Rienzo proclaimed the ancient majesty of the Roman people. The ceremony of knighthood took place on the first day of August. On the same day he also summoned the emperor and the electors to appear in Rome. On the next day he celebrated the festival of the unity of Italy and presented the standards. About this time, too, he received

Parallel Source Problems in Medieval History

a request from Joanna of Naples, who was in trouble for the murder of her husband, to have Rienzo decide her case. The king of Hungary, who was trying to avenge the death of that husband, also appealed to him, while the powerful dukes of southern Italy entreated his good-will. On the 15th of that month he was crowned with the six crowns. Murmurs of opposition began to arise at Avignon and spread southward. The nobles, awaiting the first opportunity to overthrow the plebeian upstart, began to conspire against him. Some of them he lured to a banquet on the 14th of September, where he took them captive. But, although he had condemned them to death, he let them go three days later, for which he paid dearly. On the 19th of the month he broached his definite plans for Italian unity to the cities of Italy. The papal vicar was dismissed from office, but the net began to draw more closely about Rienzo. The papal legate from Sicily was ordered to Rome. On the 7th of October he was empowered to depose him, and five days later he was given definite instructions of procedure. Letters had meanwhile been sent to various states and nobles in the neighborhood to give the legate aid, and the Roman nobles were the first to arise. The legate arrived in Rome and summoned Rienzo. But the tribune overawed him for the moment, and momentarily, too, was successful over the nobles in a battle on the 20th of November. They continued, however, to ravage the territory outside of Rome, and papal opposition grew stronger. On the 3d of December he was excommunicated. On the 15th of that month he publicly abdicated and withdrew to the castle of St. Angelo, where he hid for a time.

Later he withdrew as a fugitive, and little was known about him in the next two years. In 1350 he appeared at the court of Charles IV., king of Germany, whom he urged to come to Rome as the savior of the Roman Empire. But Charles kept him in genteel imprisonment for the next two years, although the pope made numerous requests for the prisoner. Finally, in 1352, he was with reluctance given over to the papacy. At Avignon he was kept in chains, and in imminent danger of being put to death, but with the death of Clement VI. and the accession of Innocent VI. a different solution was found. He was sent with the fighting cardinal, Albornoz, to subdue the papal states. The work was successful, and Rienzo was rewarded with the position of senator of Rome, but his local enemies brought that office to a short end by killing him October 8, 1354.

II. THE AUTHORS OF THE ACCOUNTS

This problem differs from the preceding in that it is not so much a comparison of several authors describing the same event as it is a comparison of the attitude of the same writers toward an event at different times. The following selections are taken mainly from the letters of Rienzo and the pope, Clement VI., and have, therefore, largely the character of official documents. These letters, though addressed to one person only, were usually intended to be read by several, which is especially true of Rienzo's letters. The pompous, grandiloquent style of the latter, with the long, involved sentences and parenthetical clauses, requires painstaking study to understand them fully. Occasionally the unusually long sentences of the original have been broken up for the purposes of this translation, but so far as convenient the original form has been preserved. The papal letters are only less involved than those of Rienzo, and both represent a more ornate Latin than that used by the earlier

Parallel Source Problems in Medieval History

medieval chroniclers. Only portions of some of the original letters are here translated; those parts which deal with the events that occurred at Rome between the first and the fifteenth days of August, 1347. The other matters, relating to the struggles with the nobles or the tribune's other activities, have been omitted as far as possible.

1. *The Titles Used by Cola di Rienzo.* These titles are taken from Rienzo's own letters, and are almost entirely of his own conception. For this reason they cast an interesting light upon the character of the man himself, and the changes which they undergo in the course of the year assume an almost pathetic significance.

2. *Letter of Clement VI. to Raymond, Bishop of Orvieto, and Cola di Rienzo.* This letter was written June 27, 1347, and practically all of this is here translated. It is self-explanatory, and is particularly valuable for the papal attitude at this time. The papal letter of October 12th throws some additional light on this point.

3. *Letter of Rienzo to the Commune of Florence.* This is a copy of a circular letter written July 9th to the cities around Rome. Congratulations had been received in various forms from many people, even from the pope; his plans had been unusually successful; and he was now ready to stage an elaborate coronation. The letter is translated in full.

4. *Letter of Rienzo to a Friend at Avignon.* Only a part of this letter, which was written July 15th, is here translated. The other portions deal with the various events that have happened under Rienzo's administration. This is practically the first official announcement of the coming celebration to the pope. Notice the indirect way in which it is given.

5. *Vita Anonymi di Cola di Rienzo* (*Anonymous Life of*

The Coronation of Cola di Rienzo

Cola di Rienzo). Who the author of this life was is not definitely known, but there seems little doubt that he was a personal witness of most of the events of Rienzo's public career. He wrote his account just after the death of the tribune in a dialect form of Italian intended probably for general reading. Though crude in language and style, it is very graphic, and by historians is usually regarded as a very impartial account. The last paragraph about the death of Rienzo is added for its side light on the author of the account.

6. *The Citation of the German Emperor and Electors.* This document, which was made public on the first day of August, had been previously prepared, and represents perhaps the most ambitious undertaking of the tribune. Those cited did not appear.

7. *Letter of Rienzo to Clement VI.* This letter has two dates—the first part was written presumably on July 27th, the rest of it August 5th. Only parts of it are here translated, but the rest of it deals in the same happy way with the happenings at Rome and Rienzo's plans. A delicate question might arise as to whether he intended this to reach the pope at the original date.

8. *Giovanni Villani: Historia Universalis.* This writer died in 1348, a victim to the black death which was sweeping over Europe at that time. He lived at Florence, where he was engaged during the years before his death in writing a history of his own times. Experience in the extensive commercial and diplomatic relations of his city and his shrewd judgment enabled him to write an unusually complete and sound history of his times. On Roman affairs he was very well informed, though he was not an eye-witness, and his account is here valuable as the estimate of Rienzo by an expert and close observer at the time.

Parallel Source Problems in Medieval History

9. *The Program of the Coronation of Cola di Rienzo.* This document was drawn up by Rienzo himself, and contains some of the best illustrations of the mental vagaries of the famous tribune. Ancient learning and medieval allegory are closely intermingled.

10. *Letter of Clement VI. to the Papal Legate.* The pope had become alarmed by the news which he heard from Rome, and therefore wrote to the legate in Sicily to take measures to check Rienzo's career. The letter is dated at Avignon, August 21st. Only the charges against Rienzo have been here translated.

11. *Letter of Rienzo to Clement VI.* The exact date of this letter is lost, but it was probably written some time between the 15th and 31st of August. From various sources Rienzo learned of the opposition to him at Avignon, and in the letter which is here translated he replies to the charges. Notice the confident yet anxious tone.

12. *Letter of Rienzo to Rinaldo Orsini at Avignon.* Momentary successes gave him added confidence, and in this letter to the papal notary he recounted what had happened, and in a facetious, almost insolent way he treats the charges again. The latter part is here given. It is dated September 17th.

13. *Letter of Rienzo to the City of Florence.* This is a copy of another circular letter addressed to the cities of Italy, and was written only two days after the preceding letter. In this he broached more clearly his plans for Italian unity.

14. *Letter of Rienzo to Clement VI.* The definite opposition of the pope had become evident even to Rienzo himself, and practically all of this letter, written October 11th, is devoted to a serious defense of himself. Only portions of the letter are here given.

15. *Letter of Clement VI. to the Papal Legate.* This is

The Coronation of Cola di Rienzo

the last of a number of vigorous letters sent by the pope to the legate and other adherents in Italy, and sums up rather fully the charges against Rienzo, as well as conveying definite instructions of procedure against him. It was sent from Avignon, October 12th, and the legate almost immediately left Sicily to come to Rome.

16. *Letter of Clement to the People of Rome.* The pope had decided to oust Rienzo. This letter, sent December 3d, is practically a bull of excommunication against Rienzo. The tribune abdicated December 15, 1347.

III. SUGGESTED QUESTIONS FOR STUDY

1. What was the general attitude toward Rienzo before August 1, 1347?
2. Whence did Rienzo derive his power?
3. What position did the papal vicar have at Rome in the pope's opinion?
4. What position did the papal vicar have at Rome in Rienzo's opinion?
5. Describe the various steps in the knighting of Rienzo.
6. By what authority did he re-establish the majesty of the Roman people?
7. What object did he have in citing the emperor and the electors?
8. What evidence do you find to show that he also cited the pope?
9. What was the relation of Rienzo to the pope in Rienzo's opinion?
10. What was the papal opinion of that relationship?
11. How did Rienzo assure himself that he was not opposing the church?
12. Did the papal vicar approve of Rienzo's acts?
13. What steps did Rienzo take to bring about Italian unity?
14. Whence did Rienzo get his ideas about his positions?
15. Did he have any ambition of becoming emperor?

Parallel Source Problems in Medieval History

16. For what reason did the pope oppose Rienzo?
17. Which do you regard as the most important reason for papal opposition?
18. What information do you gain from these documents about the office of syndic?
19. What evidence do you find to show that the expectation of the Jubilee in 1350 played any part in the career of Rienzo?
20. Describe the character of Rienzo.

IV. The Sources

1. *Titles Used by Cola di Rienzo.*

Nicolaus Laurentii.

Nicolaus Laurentii, Magistratus Maiori Cameræ Urbis.

Nicolaus, Severus et Clemens, Libertatis, Pacis Iustitiæque Tribunus, et Sacræ Romanæ Reipublicæ Liberator Illustris.

Candidatus Spiritus Sancti, Miles, Nicolaus, Severus et Clemens, Liberator Urbis, Zelator Italiæ, Amator Orbis et Tribunus Augustus.

Nicolaus, Tribunus Augustus.

Nicolaus, Tribunus.

These six titles were all employed by Rienzo to designate himself and his position in the year 1347. The first was his name—Nicholas, son of Lawrence. This designation he used but rárely. The second describes his position as notary, though the title given

him by Clement was "NOTARIUS CAMERÆ URBIS."
The third title he assumed after his accession to the
tribunate on the 20th of May, and it appears consistently in his letters until the improvement on the
first day of August, which is the fourth title cited.
In the letter to Clement on the 11th of October
the fifth title appears, and was used as late as the
2nd of December, though the sixth title seems to be
all that he saved from the wreck. To it he clung
until he came back to Rome in 1354.

2. *Letter of Clement VI. to Bishop Raymond and Cola di Rienzo* (June 27, 1347).

Clement, Bishop, . . . to the venerable brother
Raymond, bishop of Orvieto, our vicar in
the spiritual affairs of the City, and to the
beloved son Nicholas, son of Lawrence, citizen of Rome, our servant, rectors of the said
city and district, greetings.

Among other things dear to our heart, we desire
with ardent wishes that the insolence of the many be
restrained and the renowned city, its people and inhabitants, who lie close to the heart of ourselves and
the apostolic seat, should be happy with an abundance
of peace and security in the cultivation of faith and
justice. It has, indeed, just come to the hearing
of our apostolate by verbal as well as by written
account that the many excesses and insolence, which
were disturbing the peace and welfare [of the City]
not a little, have been suppressed, and that on the

The Coronation of Cola di Rienzo

vigil of the feast of the Pentecost just past, the said people came to the Capitol of the same City and in the hope that the welfare of the said City could, with the Divine and our favor aiding you, be cared for through your circumspect and faithful diligence, did unanimously and heartily choose you as rectors of that City and district, confident of our good will in this matter. Consider prudently the fact that in time past, at the beginning of our promotion to the apex of the highest apostolate, the aforesaid people, with free will and of their own accord, granted the offices of senator, captain, syndic, and the other offices of the oft-mentioned City, as pertain to them, to us during our life-time; and [you] receive the office of such rectory in the name of and to the honor of ourselves and the Roman church. As you have exercised that [office], continue to exercise it diligently.

Since, therefore, the above and certain other matters, more seriously explained, have been more fully made known to us, and since, as numerous people have pleasingly asserted to us, many and various boons have accrued and are accruing constantly to the same City, district, and the neighboring regions also through your administration with that same regard for the cultivation of justice, and in order that boons of this kind may continue and, as we very much wish, likewise increase, we appoint you as rectors of the aforesaid City and district by the contents of these presents until such a time as we ordain otherwise in regard to these matters, and grant you full power of enacting, executing, commanding, decreeing, and exercising one and all the powers which pertain to an office of this kind. Wherefore we command your discretion by these apostolic writings, that this, which you have laudably received, as is above stated, you do laudably carry out, and, laying aside all partiality whatsoever, do so observe and cause to be observed the cultivation of justice, faith, and peace in that same City, its districts and possessions, that from your administration, with the assistance of the Divine favor, the hoped for fruits may accrue, and that you may thence not unworthily acquire the Divine favor of ourselves and the apostolic seat in greater measure.

Dated at Avignon, on the fifth day before the Calends of July, in the sixth year of our pontificate.

3. *The Letter of Rienzo to the Commune of Florence* (July 9, 1347).

With our most clement Lord Jesus Christ as author, Nicholas, stern and clement, tribune of liberty, peace, and justice, and illustrious liberator of the sacred Roman republic, to the splendid and powerful, the potesta, captain, council, and commune of the city of Florence, the especial and beloved sons and friends of the sacred Roman people, greetings, peace, and an abundance of joy.

The Coronation of Cola di Rienzo

For the honor of the beloved City, which is the capital of the cities of the world and all sacred Italy, and with the name and favor of the Holy Ghost, from whom our honor took its beginning and receives continual addition, we are arranging to be promoted on the Calends of August, next to be, to the glorious knighthood by the syndics of the sacred Roman people and also by the syndics of the other cities and lands of the same sacred Italy. Subsequently, on the festival of the most glorious Virgin Mary in the same month [August 15th] we are preparing to be crowned with the tribunitian laurel under the title of liberty, peace, and justice, and we beseech your magnificent and dearest friendship, which we embrace with a special zeal of affection and which we know delights in our joys, that it please you to send ambassadors and syndics properly empowered for this purpose to renew the ancient friendship and participate with us in so solemn a festival of our joys.

Dated in the Capitol, where we flourish with upright heart in a rule of justice (on the ninth day of July), fifteenth Indiction, in the first year of the liberated republic.

4. *Letter of Rienzo to a Friend at Avignon* (July 15, 1347).

DEAREST FRIEND,— . . . And God, to whom all things are disclosed, knows that not ambition for the dignity, fame, or honor of the office, nor for worldly gold (which I have always abhorred as filth, but desire for the common good of the whole republic and its most sanctified condition), induced us to bend our neck to so heavy a yoke as has been placed upon our shoulders, not by man, but by God. He knows if such an office was obtained with prayers by us; if we have conferred offices, benefices, and honors upon our relatives; if we have accumulated wealth for ourselves; if we have departed from the truth; if we hold men by words; if we make disposition for ourselves, or our heirs; if we delight in the sweetness of foods or any other voluptuous pleasure; and, if we do anything that is pretended. God is our witness, too, for the things we have done and are doing for the poor, widows, and orphans. Cola the son of Lawrence used to live more quietly than Cola the tribune. . . . Nay, on the witness of the Holy Ghost and the blessed apostles, in no hour of the day can we obtain rest, but add even the night to work and labor. . . .

Know likewise that to the despite and disgrace of John de Vico,[1] the most wicked traitor, we have received from the Roman people the office of prefect of the city. We add to this pleasure [the news] that, in the name of God, we intend, on the Calends of

---

[1] The office of prefect of the city was a feudal office of importance in the city and neighborhood of Rome. It had been granted originally by the emperor and later by the pope. John of Vico held out against Rienzo for some time, but on July 16th he made an abject surrender. Rienzo then received the office.

The Coronation of Cola di Rienzo

August next to be, the pontifical and imperial day,[1] to be promoted to knighthood by the Roman people, with the grace of the Holy Ghost. And when we are thus knight of the Holy Ghost we have arranged to be crowned, on the festival of the glorious Virgin Mary in the same month, with the tribunitian laurel which tribunes of ancient times were wont to assume. Likewise we shall not fear to imitate the customs of those who, though promoted to office from the plow, returned again to the plow when their administration was ended.

Do you inform the reverend father, Lord R. [inaldi] of the sons of Orsini, the notary of the lord pope, concerning all these things, for he has written to us very much, and we have not as yet had a chance to write back to him. But do you excuse us to him that, if we do not now write to him, it is because of the press of the coming event.

Do you also, dearest, strive to hasten your return, for we are providing for you an honorable and good office, since you know that we do not easily, neither by simony, by prayers, nor other extraneous influence, accept officials, but we promote to office men of proven worth on the basis of virtue.

Dated at the Capitol, where we flourish with up-

[1] In the days of the Roman Empire the "Feriæ Augusti" were celebrated on the first day of August. Later the Christian Church held the festival of St. Peter on the same day. The chains with which Peter was supposed to have been held captive were publicly exhibited on this day.

right heart in a rule of justice, on the fifteenth day
of July, fifteenth Indiction, in the first year of the
liberated republic.

5. *Vita Anonymi di Cola di Rienzo* (*Anonymous
Life of Cola di Rienzo*).

We are going to describe the manner in which
Nicholas received the knighthood. When, according to general opinion, everything had turned out
favorably for himself, and when he had without
obstacle and in peace assumed the rule which he had
wished for, he aspired to the honorable rank of
knight. On the evening of the festival of the
Blessed Virgin Mary, about the middle of August,
he was made Knight of the Bath.[1] The ceremony
was conducted in this manner. In the first place, he
made arrangements for the feast to be given in connection with the ceremony in the Pontifical Palace
and in the adjacent houses of the Church of St. John
on the Lateran. Tables were made from the floor-work and wooden inclosures of the homes of the
barons of the city. Many days before the feast he
had these same tables set in the ancient hall of the
old Palace of Constantine, in the Papal Palace, and
in the New Palace, to the wonder and amazement of

---

[1] The bath of knighthood was not an unusual procedure in the installation of Roman officials. In 1326 two nobles of the Colonna and Orsini families were compelled to take such a bath in rose-water, and were then raised to their new offices by the people. The title of Knight of the Bath has many parallels in the history of chivalry.

The Coronation of Cola di Rienzo

all. In order to provide more commodious entrances and exits for the wooden ladders which he had ordered built so that the food might be conveniently carried in from the kitchen, he had some of the walls of these old palaces cut down. In one corner of the halls he had a wine cellar prepared.

Then on the vigil of the feast of St. Peter ad Vincula, at the ninth hour, the whole city, men and women alike, thronged under the colonnades at the Temple of St. John and sought a standing place, each for himself. The people filled the public roads to see this ceremony. Soon there came an innumerable host of men of various nations and peoples, all mounted. Barons, magistrates of the city, and officials of the forum, each garbed in silks and bearing standards, were mounted upon horses from whose chests hung tinkling bells and which pranced about in amusing fashion. They were followed by clowns and pantomimists without number who kept up a continual din with horns, trumpets, pipes, and little trumpets. After these came the wife and mother of the tribune accompanied by several worthy matrons for the sake of dignity. Two youths of comely appearance preceded the wife of Nicholas and held the gold-painted bridle of her noble horse. Then with a loud flare of silver trumpets and the sound of many flutes there came a band of horsemen, who flashed their spears sportively as they rode. Among these the Cornetani and the Perusini excelled the rest. Then came the tribune with the vicar of the pope clinging to his side. Before the tribune rode a man holding in his hand an unsheathed sword, while yet another carried a banner, which he held over the head of the tribune. Nicholas, bearing in his hand a steel scepter and surrounded by an attendance of many nobles, was garbed in a silken cloak of wonderful whiteness embroidered by needle with golden twisted threads.

Toward evening of that day he ascended to the chapel of Pope Boniface and addressed the people, saying, "Let it be known to you that this very night I shall receive the ornaments of knighthood. Tomorrow when you return I shall explain to you something which will be pleasing to the Power in Heaven and to men on Earth." In a throng so large and of such a character there were no quarrels among the armed men. Not even murmurs arose: the minds of all were filled with joy. Even when two men had provoked each other with angry words and had drawn their swords, they did not come to blows, but sheathed their steel and turned peacefully to their own affairs. People had flocked to this celebration from the nearby towns, nay even the old men, girls, widows, and wives.

When all had left, the clerk solemnly read the mass, and when he was through the tribune proceeded into the bath. There in the precious font of stone

The Coronation of Cola di Rienzo

which the emperor Constantine used,[1] he was sprinkled with water. This doubtless afforded all an opportunity for admiration, but also for saying many things. Then the tribune was girt with a sword by the lord Vico Scotto, a knight, citizen of Rome, after which ceremony he went to sleep on a magnificent bed within the circle of columns in that place which is called the Font of St. John. Here he lay throughout the night. And I have heard of a strange omen. When the tribune had climbed into that bed which had just recently been built with every necessary prop, a part of it suddenly fell to earth and so remained during the whole silent night. With the coming of the day he arose and was adorned with a beautiful cloak trimmed with leopard's fur. The sword with which Vico Scotto had girded him he wore at his side, while on his heels were golden spurs. With these insignia of knighthood he proceeded again into public. The City of Rome and all the knighthood flocked to the Temple of St. John. Barons, pleaders, and citizens all were there to see lord Nicholas, son of Lawrence, the knight. Lord Nicholas as a knight, surrounded by a famous following, was present at the most solemn sacrifice of the mass which was celebrated in the chapel of

---

[1] There was an unfounded legend that Constantine had been baptized and miraculously cured of his leprosy by Pope Sylvester. The stone basin in which this is believed to have occurred still stands in the Baptistry of the Church of St. John in Rome.

Parallel Source Problems in Medieval History

Pope Boniface. All the ornaments were displayed, while up in a gallery a band played music. The celebration went on as follows. The tribune appeared before the people, and in a loud voice said, "We summon the Lord Pope Clement to betake himself back to Rome, his own seat." Then he summoned the college of cardinals, likewise Lewis of Bavaria[1] and the electors of the German emperor, and said, "Let them come and show by what right they choose an emperor." For he found it written that after the lapse of a certain time the right of election reverts to the hands of the Roman people. When he had finished the summons, he immediately despatched couriers with letters to this effect. Then, drawing his sword and slashing the air through the three directions of the earth, he said, "This is mine; this is mine; this is mine."

To all of these acts the vicar of the pope was a witness, tolerating each like a fool or an idiot. He did not seem to know the meaning of it all and seemed stupefied at the strangeness. Nevertheless, he protested. With the voice and strength of the notary who accompanied him, he denounced it publicly, saying, "These things which the tribune has done, he has perpetrated not only without the will and

---

[1] Ludwig of Bavaria, who had been elected by the princes of Germany as their king and had been crowned emperor by the Roman people, had been excommunicated by the pope, and Charles of Bohemia had been chosen king in 1346. Hence the crime of Rienzo in calling him Duke of Bavaria.

The Coronation of Cola di Rienzo

knowledge of the vicar, but also without the assent of the pope." Then he asked the notary to make public the text of the written denunciation. While the notary was raising his voice to make the protest of the vicar known to the people, the lord Nicholas ordered the trumpeters, flute players and cornetists to strike up the sounds of their instruments that by this greater noise he might prevent the lesser strength of the notary's voice from being heard. In this way the lone voice of the notary was confused and overcome by the overwhelming noise of the musicians. In fact, there was a sly laugh of derision.

When these things were thus being done, the mass was brought to an end. It is worthy of observation that on that day from dawn till evening there flowed, without ceasing, red wine through the right, water through the left opening of the nostrils of the bronze horse of Constantine. Leaden pipes had been previously prepared for this purpose. All the youths, citizens, and visitors alike who were thirsty gathered around and drank joyfully and festively. The fact that the tribune had bathed in the font of Constantine and had summoned the pope left the people very undecided as to just what to make of his actions. Some blamed Nicholas for rashness, others for haste, still others for foolhardiness.

He, however, together with most of the nobles, repaired to the tables, sumptuously laden with a great variety of foods and the best of wines. At the marble table, which is the pontifical table, the lord Nicholas and the papal vicar ate alone. The old hall of St. John was everywhere filled with tables. The wife of the tribune and the other women had their feast in the hall of the new pontifical palace. The feast was characterized by a scarcity of water rather than of wine, and it was free to any one who cared to eat. No particular order was observed in the seating of the guests, abbots, clerics, merchants, and others all being seated at the same table. There was a supply of sweetmeats there to suit varied tastes; starlings, the most delicious of fish; pheasants and kid. No one was forbidden to carry home the remains of the feast if they so desired. The legates who had come from the different cities to see the tribune were invited to the feast, in the course of which one of the crowd of mimics, dressed in the hide of a bull and looking not unlike one, cavorted around. When the feast was at an end, Cola, dressed in his cloak trimmed with leopard skins and accompanied by a large body of horsemen, returned to the Capitol. This was done with unusual silence because the tribune had so ordered it at his assumption of knighthood. He had constructed for himself a chest at the top of which was an opening, and which had never since been of use to any one. Besides, he has made a beautiful cap, set with pearls, at the top of which there appeared a little dove of pearls. Such faults of various kinds opened up the chasm for Cola and hastened him to perdition.

. . . . . .

Such was the end of Cola di Rienzo, who had made himself tribune augustus and defender of the Roman people. In his chamber they found a steel mirror, very highly polished and engraved with many characters and figures, within which he held an evil spirit enticed from Hell. Besides this they found a writing table on which he had written the names of Romans and the tribute which he had decided to levy upon them. Upon 100 men of the first rank he had set a tribute of 500 florins; upon 100 of the second rank 400 florins; of the third class 100 florins; of the fourth class 50; and of the fifth class 10 florins. In the present year of our Lord, 1354, on the 8th day of September of the 3d hour, Nicholas was killed by the wrath of the people. The visitors and foreigners allied with him were despoiled of their goods, their arms, and their horses. Those who were in Rome at the time and the others stationed for fighting purposes in the fortress just outside the City were sent away stripped of their possessions.

6. *Citation of the German Emperor and Electors* (August 1, 1347).

To the honor and glory of the highest God the Father, Son, and Holy Ghost, and of the blessed apostles Peter and Paul, of St. John the Baptist, in whose most holy temple we received baptism, in the

Parallel Source Problems in Medieval History

font forsooth' of the most holy prince of glorious memory, the lord Constantine, the most Christian and august emperor; also the glorious bath of knighthood, with the effulgent title of the Holy Ghost, whose unworthy servant and knight we are.

We, candidate of the Holy Ghost, knight Nicholas, stern and clement, liberator of the City, zealot of Italy, lover of the world and tribune augustus, wishing and desiring that the gift of the Holy Ghost be received and increased in the city as well as throughout all Italy, and we imitating, as much as we are permitted by God, the good will, kindness, and liberality of the ancient Roman princes, make known to all, that long ago, after we had assumed the office of tribune, the Roman people learned again on the advice of each and all the judges, wise men and advocates of the City that it still has that authority, power, and jurisdiction in the whole world which it had in the beginning and which it had when the aforesaid city was at its height; and it has expressly revoked all privileges made to the prejudice of such right, authority, power, and jurisdiction.

We, therefore, on account of the ancient authority, power, and jurisdiction and the present power granted to us by the Roman people in public parliament and by our Lord, the highest pontiff, recently, as is manifest from his public and apostolic bulls, in order that we may not seem to the Roman people as well as to the aforesaid people of sacred Italy in any

The Coronation of Cola di Rienzo

way ungrateful or avaricious of the grace of the Holy
Ghost, and that we may not through negligence
permit the rights and jurisdiction of the Roman
people to be further lost, do with the authority and
grace of God and the Holy Ghost and in every way,
right, and form, decree, declare, and pronounce the
holy Roman City, the capital of the world and the
foundation of the Christian faith, and the states of
Italy, one and all, to be free. We have and do give
the same the security of full liberty, and the individual peoples of the whole sacred Italy we decree to
be free. And from now on we make, declare, and
pronounce all the aforesaid peoples and citizens of
the cities of Italy Roman citizens, and we wish them
to enjoy the privilege of Roman liberty in addition.

Likewise, with the same authority of God and the
Holy Ghost, and of the aforesaid Roman people, we
say, confess, and also declare that the election of the
Roman Emperor, the jurisdiction and monarchy of
the entire holy empire pertains to that beloved city
and its people and also to the whole sacred Italy;
that to them it has devolved legitimately for many
causes and reasons which we will cause to be declared in their place and time. For one and all the
prelates, emperors elect and electors, kings, dukes,
princes, counts, margraves, people, associations, and
any others, who are in particular or in common of any
prominence whatsoever, who wish to gainsay this
or pretend authority and power in the aforesaid

election and in the empire itself, we assign and fix in these writings, the period from now to the feast of the Pentecost, next to be, that within the said limit of time they should appear with their claims before us and other officials of the lord pope and the Roman people in the beloved City and the sacrosanct Church of the Lateran: otherwise, we shall proceed onward from the aforesaid limit according to right and as the Holy Ghost shall minister. And none the less, in addition to all the aforesaid, we do cause to be cited in particular the illustrious princes mentioned below, the lord Ludwig of Bavaria, the lord Charles, King of Bohemia, who assert that they are emperors of the Romans; the lord duke of Bavaria, the lord duke of Austria, the lord margrave of Brandenburg, the lord archbishop of Mainz, the lord archbishop of Treves, the lord archbishop of Cologne, the lord duke of Saxony; that they should appear personally before us and the other officials of the lord our pope and of the Roman people in the said city and place within the aforesaid limit of time; otherwise, we will proceed as is stated above, their absence and refusal to appear notwithstanding. . . .

In the fifteenth Indiction, on the first day of August, the aforesaid were made public before the Roman people and approved by that people present in the court of the Church of the Lateran, in the presence of the lord vicar of the lord pope. . . .

The Coronation of Cola di Rienzo

7. *Letter of Rienzo to Clement VI.* (July 27–August 5, 1347).

. . . And after I have received the knighthood, I am arranging on the festival of Holy Mary in the month of August to be crowned with the tribunitian laurel which was wont in ancient times to be given to the tribunes as a mark of honor. And just as it was no disgrace for them who had been promoted to honors from the plow to return to the plow when their administration was at an end, so I will not be ashamed to return to my writing tablet as before. But I desire your holiness to know that as I know my shoulders are feeble for the burden of so great an office, a burden which is ever increasing, I have already twice proposed in full council that the office of this administration should end with one term of three months and that a new official should be placed in that office, urging this for many reasons and because many citizens might then become worthy by practice in offices of this kind. Yet, most holy father, all at that council, this one tearing his clothes, another with eyes flowing in tears, another disfiguring his face with his nails, all shouted together for grief, "We will die, every one of us, before we will have any other administration than yours. For we have by our destruction and servitude experienced the quality of another régime sufficiently, and it is apparent to our eyes that the Holy Ghost is working so many miracles in this City through yours that we are and will live in such days in justice, peace, and the sweetest liberty." Therefore, most holy father, I must remain to do with thought and deed whatever my devotion for the obedience and honor of the holy church and your most clement holiness may be able to do. And I supplicate you in reverence that you may deem it worthy before God to command your present and future officials in the Patrimony and Campagna to remain constant in law and virtue and not permit themselves against this condition to be deceived by the wiles and blandishments of the Roman magnates who are eager to absorb your beloved city. For, yesterday, the captain of the Patrimony who was aiding the enemy of God and the church against the city and its present condition died suddenly just as if, nay assuredly, God were the avenger and the Blessed Apostles Peter and Paul, whose cause is involved, cooperated. And I believe without doubt and with a most certain hope in God, whose judgments are hidden, every one will fare thus who presumes to oppose this holy condition . . .

MOST HOLY FATHER AND MOST CLEMENT LORD,—And since the sending of these letters has been delayed by the tardiness of the messenger after they had been dated, I make known to your holiness that on the Calends of August, the pontifical and imperial day, in the Church of the Lateran, the Holy Ghost

The Coronation of Cola di Rienzo

deigned to promote me, though unworthy, to knighthood at the hands of all the prelates of the City and also of the knights of that beloved City and of the syndics of the City, of Tuscany and the neighboring cities; that, in the stone font in which Constantine was baptized, I received the bath of knighthood; that in an assembly of all the people of the city and countless men of other cities, as it proceeds from the Holy Ghost, I received to the citizenship of the City all the cities of Tuscany with the consent of your venerable vicar in the city who assisted us in everything; and, that in a general edict, I cited one and all the elected, electors, and whoever else pretended to any right in the election of the Roman Empire and in the Empire itself to appear in the City with their claims before your vicar and myself and the Roman people before the festival of the Pentecost next to be; otherwise, procedure will be taken in the business of the election itself, as shall be according to the law. Since, however, the respectable and pure providence of the Holy Ghost has induced me to make such a citation, in order that such disturbance of the elected and electors may create an uncertainty of strength among them, and the very uncertainty itself force them to recur to the holy Roman Church and your holiness with greater reverence, nay more, that they may regard God, the said see, and your holiness more devoutly and reverently and that the unholy clash of armed men, and most savage shedding of Christian blood may end and peace flourish everywhere, the especial and honorable message of the ambassadors of your Roman people and mine is being sent to your holiness, to the kings of the Franks and English and to every other king of the Catholic faith, to the prominent dukes and princes as well as to the aforesaid elected and electors. For I shall continue to do all things with reverence and honor for your holiness, and from these I shall not desist as long as I have life. And with the aid of the Holy Ghost a certain hope warns me that, in the Jubilee year of the Lord, your holiness will be in Rome and the Emperor with you, that there will be one flock and one shepherd, through the unity of the same grace of the Holy Ghost. For the rest, since the wide-spread favor of the Holy Ghost has within a few days freed and enlarged the republic under my administration, and my humble self was, on the Calends of the aforesaid August, promoted to knighthood, the name and title of Augustus, as it is below written, has been assigned to me.

Dated as above on the fifth day of August.

The humble creature, candidate of the Holy Ghost . . .

And since for a detailed account of the things which the Spirit of the Lord is doing for the growth of this office, a secretary does not suffice and the amount of one leaf yields to the magnitude of the affair, I,

The Coronation of Cola di Rienzo

your humble little servant and creature, dare with friendly and domestic assurance write to your holiness on a supplementary leaf, and I desire you to know that, at the festival when knighthood was conferred upon my humble self, by the grace of the Holy Ghost, ambassadors of Florence, Sienna, Perugia, and of all the great cities of Italy met in the City. I [cultivated] them through eagerly sought rings as a sign of love and charity and for the strengthening of perpetual unity under the faith, reverence, and honor of the holy mother of Church and of you. I also conferred these standards upon the cities mentioned below, namely: upon the city of Perugia the standard of the emperor Constantine, of happy memory; upon Sienna a standard of liberty; upon Florence a standard of Italy; upon Todi a standard of my name; [each standard] being received with the greatest alacrity by the ambassadors above mentioned. . . .

. . . for whatever may be done, has been done and will be done in the future, it is and will be to the honor and praise of your holiness and the exaltation of the Church, under whose reverence I humbly walk, and devoutly advance to do in every single thing as the Holy Ghost shall grant. . . .

8. *Giovanni Villani: Historia Universalis* (*Universal History*).

In this year, 1347, on the 20th day of May, the day of the Pentecost—there having returned to Rome one Niccolaus di Rienzo, who had gone to the court of the pope for the Roman people to plead that he [the pope] with his court should come back to stay at the Seat of St. Peter as he ought, and the pope having given good but vain promises—they summoned a parliament in Rome to which many people had congregated, and in which he [Cola] made known his mission with pleasing and ornate words like one who was master of rhetoric. And as he had arranged with certain of the leaders of the plebeians, with a shout he was made tribune of the people. . . .

. . . And from the present government which had been made he took the rule and office entirely from the nobility of Rome and its vicinity and caused some of the chief men who had carried on depredations in Rome and its vicinity to be captured. He caused stern justice to be done, and drove out certain of the Orsini and Colonna and the other nobles of Rome and all the others who had not already gone to their lands and castles to escape the wrath of the tribune and the people. Their fortresses the tribune seized. . . . And in a short time, through his stern justice, Rome and the surrounding lands were in such a state of security that one could go about safely there by night and day. He sent letters also to all the chief cities of Italy and one to our commune with many excellent sayings. And then he sent to us five solemn ambassadors who glorified themselves, and then our commune, both as

The Coronation of Colá di Rienzo

if our city was a child of Rome and an edifice founded by the Roman people, and asked for aid for their army. To these ambassadors great honor was accorded; 100 knights were sent to the tribune, and more were promised if necessary. The people of Perugia sent some. Then on the day of St. Peter ad Vincula, namely, the first day of August, as he had signified through his letters and ambassadors, he was made knight by the syndic of the people of Rome at the altar of St. Peter: and first, through pomp, he bathed at the Lateran in the stone font, in that very one in which the emperor Constantine bathed when St. Sylvester healed him of leprosy. And when the grand banquet and feast of the knighthood was over and the people had been summoned, he made a great address, telling how he wished to restore all Italy to the obedience of Rome in the ancient manner, maintaining the City in its liberty and justice. Then he caused certain new banners which he had made to be brought forth . . . and he caused the syndic of the commune of Florence to be called forth to take it; the syndic not appearing, he had it placed at the altar upon a staff and said, "Verily, they will take it at the time and place," and many other banners he gave to the syndics of the other cities in the neighborhood and vicinity of Rome. And on the same day he had the lord of Corneto, who had robbed the country around Rome, hanged. When this had been done he had, by voice in this parliament and by his letters, cited the electors of the empire of Germany and Ludwig of Bavaria, he who had been made emperor, and Charles of Bohemia, who had recently been made emperor, to come to Rome between that time and Pentecost to explain their election and show by what right they had had themselves called emperors, and the electors to show by what authority they had elected them. And then he had brought forth and made public certain privileges of the pope as though he had a commission from him to do it. We will leave for a little while the strange and grand undertakings of the new tribune of Rome, to all of which we can come back in time (provided that his signory and rank have power), as well as all that was said by the wise and discreet men up to that time to the effect that this undertaking of the tribune was a fantastic work and one of short duration.

9. *Program of the Coronation of Cola di Rienzo.*

The coronation of the tribune proceeded as follows: The first crown was of oak, and was presented by the prior of the Lateran Church, with the words, "Accept this crown of oak, since you preserve the citizens from death."

The second crown was of ivy, and was presented by the prior of the Church of St. Peter, with the words, "Accept this crown of ivy, since you love religion."

The third crown was of myrtle, and was presented

The Coronation of Cola di Rienzo

by the deacon of the Church of St. Paul, with the words, "Accept this crown of myrtle, since you cherish your office and learning, and hate avarice."

The fourth crown was of laurel, and was presented by the abbot of St. Lawrence beyond the Walls, with the words, "Accept this laurel, since you cherish your office and learning, and hate avarice."[1]

The fifth crown was of olive, and was presented by the prior of the Church of Maria Maggiore, with the words, "Humble sir, accept this crown of olives, since you overcome pride with humility."

The sixth crown was of silver. It, together with a scepter, was presented by the prior of the Church of the Holy Spirit on the Rocks, with the words, "Tribune Augustus, accept the gifts of the Holy Spirit, with the crown and scepter. Accept also the spiritual crown."

The apple, however, was presented by Lord Godfrey, a soldier, with the words, "Tribune Augustus, accept this apple and cultivate justice; grant liberty and peace." Then he kissed him.

The vicar of the lord of Ostia disposed of the crowns. The silver crown the archbishop of Naples did not permit to be carried away.

Throughout the ceremony the aforesaid tribune had by his side a beggar dressed in rags, as a token

---

[1] The original passage contains the same formulas for the giving of both the third and the fourth crowns, which is probably a mistake of the copyist.

of his humility, asserting that it was an ancient custom of the Roman emperors when they returned in triumph to endure patiently whatever taunts or gibes any one might cast at them that day.

10. *Letter of Clement VI. to the Papal Legate* (August 21, 1347).

After this, however, before the letters we have mentioned reached them, the aforesaid bishop and Cola directed messengers and ambassadors to us, humbly beseeching us that we should deign to confirm in the office of tribune, or grant them a new office of this kind. While we were deliberating with our brethren as to what ought to be done in this matter, we learned from the intimation and accounts of many people that the aforesaid Cola, not content with the title of rector which we had given him, styled himself tribune. Moreover, it was said that on the first day of the Calends of August just passed he took the girdle of knighthood with several fellow citizens. At the same time he fixed the day of the Assumption of the Blessed Mary just passed but then to come, for the coronation with the laurel with which he asserted the tribunes were wont to be crowned in ancient days. To such a coronation he had called the syndics of all the cities and important places of Italy; and furthermore had already begun to strike off a new coin and to make many other innovations. Among these he is said to have directed various decrees to some communities and

The Coronation of Cola di Rienzo

individuals on the lands of the church, and to have imposed unaccustomed taxes upon them, from which it seems that he is drawing them away from the dominion of the aforesaid church and is making the wealth of Rome subject to himself. . . .

11. *Letter of Rienzo to Clement VI.* (August 15–31, 1347).

MOST HOLY FATHER AND MOST MERCIFUL LORD, —That through craftiness of deceitful tongues, from which even a prophet would fain be delivered, your clemency—hitherto not easy if not, as I think, impossible to be turned from me by fallacious words, since it is written that we are not to believe everything heard—may not hold me suspected, notwithstanding the known proofs of my purity, this present letter is sent to your holiness. It is sent to declare the truth, to oppose falsehood, and to repel the craft of any person who darts arrows from his sharp tongue, like a sword, and whose innate and inveterate vice renders him unworthy not only of all dignity in the state, but also of being received into the court of your holiness.

Your holiness will have known that on the festival of the most Blessed Virgin Mary, in this present month of August, your humble servant received from the hands of the preceptor of the Hospital of the Holy Ghost, and of the vicars of the cathedral churches of the city, the . . . laurel crown which was wont of old to be given to the tribunes, and which consisted of six crowns, five of which were of natural leaves, given according to an old Roman custom to persons who had advanced the commonwealth, and the sixth of silver not exceeding the value of five gold florins; and that, after taking the above six crowns, I received also from the hands of the syndic the apple, the ensign of the army of the Roman people; all of which, in devout memory of the six gifts of the Holy Ghost, I cherished as a token of His bounty, and in acknowledgment of my reverence for the most holy Roman church and for your holiness. And in the reception of these there was no understanding of perpetual authority or infraction of power. In the full public assembly, and with the assent of the whole Roman people, very many of the syndics of all the cities of Tuscany, brothers in Christian zeal, and all those of the cities which give titles to the cardinals, were not only freed from all vassalage as to their property, but were declared by me Roman citizens, and were brought back to your authority, and to that of my lords the cardinals, whose rights had received manifest injury in consequence of the inimical nobles of this, your city. Also that no emperor, or king, or prince, or marquis, or any other under whatever title may dare to put foot in Italy without the special license of your holiness, or of the Roman people; to which I was induced by that pure and holy faith which I bear to the church, and by the

The Coronation of Cola di Rienzo

desire of peace and of the quiet of Italy and of the kingdom at large.

Likewise that no one may for the future dare to mention the detested names of Guelf and Ghibelline, but, laying aside all party distinctions, assert and acknowledge their . . . loyalty to the holy church in unity and peace. All of which and the other things done by me, if there be anything that can be esteemed contrary to the holy church, seeing that they proclaim and preach universal peace, I leave to the judgment of your holiness. I desire anxiously and unfeignedly that your holiness would deign to send hither some man of God to discuss and inquire into all those things which I have done by the will of your Roman people; and if the said man shall find any of that evil in me with which I am charged I do oblige myself, under any penalty, to be punished without mercy according to the justice of your holiness. Nor let it be unknown to your clemency that I am now proceeding with an army against the enemy of the church and of yourself, Nicholas Gartanus, formerly count of Fondi, and have already sent before me Angelo Malabreme, the chancellor of the city, to make an incursion into the lands of the said count, with 400 knights well arrayed for battle, with the grace and power of the Holy Spirit, besides 1,200 other horsemen with slingers, and an infinite number of other soldiers, who, as I hope, will easily tread him under foot, so that he shall never rise again. Of which army I have appointed John, the son of Stephen Colonna, prince of the soldiery. Because there is commencing a scarcity in those parts, although moderate, I have and, so far as I am able, am providing a remedy, by enacting that grain shall be imported from Sicily and from other countries, and by ordaining that many lands of our Roman districts, the greater part of which have lain uncultivated, shall now again be sown, for I am aware that otherwise this scarcity may increase, owing to the granting of the Jubilee, which will bring such multitudes from all the quarters to Rome, and because many have found means to amass and conceal the grain . . .

[The rest of the letter is lost.]

12. *Letter of Rienzo to Rinaldo Orsini at Avignon* (September 17, 1347).

REVEREND FATHER AND MOST BELOVED FRIEND,— Concerning the following matters do you deign to inform our lord, the highest pontiff, with a recommendation of me, his humble creature, as a suppliant. And we do not omit that all our actions after our promotion have been in the service of the holy mother church and our lord, the highest pontiff, just as also they will be. Nor is it expedient to have any care arise on this score, since it is impossible that we be turned away from this.

To these charges which are made against us in the curia about the bath of knighthood taken in the

The Coronation of Cola di Rienzo

stone font of Constantine, we say that the pagan Constantine entered the same font and was bathed there; and we believed that we, a devout Christian, and with tears honorable and virtuous, might be bathed in the same place at the hands of the vicar of the lord—our pope, for the body of our Lord is a matter of greater veneration than the font, and yet we have taken it frequently and devoutly.

If we did, with the vicar of the lord, our pope, eat at his table on which dice were formerly played and which has been afterwards always especially honored, and we did this with devotion, we do not see that we have therefore committed a fault.

However, what has been charged against us about the two-edged sword is most false, and all the charges which are made against us in the curia we leave to God for avengeance. The Roman people, too, hearing these frivolous and false charges, have held them in the greatest derision, believing nevertheless that this proceeds from an innate hatred of the nation or at the invention of those who not only desire to impede the status of the City, but are panting to utterly destroy it.

It is said that we carried on childishly. We answer that it is true that we did purely what is denounced as puerility: even God commands that the children praise him.[1]

---

[1] The translation does not bring out quite fully the play on the words "pueriliter, pure, pueritiam, and pueri," which is contained in the original.

Parallel Source Problems in Medieval History

By the whole of the Roman Province it is regarded as a matter of wonder that the Roman curia should be agitated about such things, and they say: "Would that our most holy lord and lord cardinals would see the church and the whole world in such good disposition and peace that they did not have to deal with more serious troubles." Finally we are proceeding in every single matter as the grace of the Holy Spirit directs our footsteps and disposes our acts in accordance with His will. Concerning the Jubilee, however, the Romans are not so very eager, because much labor must be done therefor.

We ask, likewise, all the clergy and all the people to pour forth devout and continual prayers to the Holy Ghost, that the Holy Ghost may deign to open and fill the heart of our lord, the highest pontiff, and the lord cardinals so that they select and place first in pure affection the fostering City filled with the bodies of the Saints and returned to justice, liberty, and peace, in preference to the city of Avignon deprived of participation in the bodies of the Saints— would that it were not of the cultivation of virtues.

13. *Letter of Rienzo to the City of Florence* (September 19, 1347).

The Candidate of the Holy Ghost, the Knight Nicholas, etc. . . .

Not without the inspiration of the same Holy Ghost we, therefore, desiring to know again the rights of the sacred Roman people, have, with the

The Coronation of Cola di Rienzo

mature consideration of those skilled in both laws, the judges of the entire college of the City, and very many others wise in the councils of sacred Italy, who knew through having turned over, discussed, and examined the expressed laws more frequently with proper comparison of opinions, said "That the senate and people of Rome have that authority and jurisdiction in the whole world which it formerly had in ancient times when it was at the height of its power, and that it can now interpret, temper, revoke, change, add to, and diminish the rights and laws, and can likewise declare and do all things as formerly, and can also revoke whatever has been done by law itself to its hurt and prejudice, and that this stood revoked by that very fact." When these matters had been discussed and known, and all, senate, magnates, men of consular rank, satraps, bishops, abbots, priors, all the clerks of the City and all the people had assembled at the sacred Lateran Palace in most full and solemn parliament, by the authority of this same people and in every way and right by which we could better proceed according to law, we declared revoked, according to the unanimous will of the entire same Roman people, all the authority, jurisdiction, and power which the senate and people of Rome had and could have, and all alienation, cession, concession, and transference of offices, dignities, powers, imperial and any other authority, given by the senate and people of Rome to whatever

men, clergy and lay, of whatever condition, and likewise of whatever nation they are, and these offices, dignities, powers, imperial and whatsoever other authority, and former and ancient rights of the same
5 Roman people we restored to ourselves and the aforementioned people. We also caused to be cited him who conducts himself as duke of Bavaria and lord Charles, illustrious king of Bohemia, who calls himself king of the Romans, as it is said, and, like
10 the preceding, other particular individuals, the elect as well as the electors, by name, and one and all emperors, kings, dukes, princes, margraves, prelates, and any others, clergy as well as laymen, who pretended to any right in the election of the empire
15 itself, and who had caused various displeasures and errors to the detriment of the City, and the whole sacred Italy, and to the subversion of the whole Christian faith. [These we cited] to appear in the City and sacred palace of the Lateran on or before
20 the festival of the Pentecost next to be, in person or through their legitimate representatives before us and the Roman people, and strive to compare all their claims in the above mentioned election and empire against the revocation itself: otherwise we
25 shall proceed in the business of such revocation and of the aforesaid imperial election as shall be according to right, their refusal to appear notwithstanding.

And in order that the gifts and favor of the Holy Ghost may be shared by all the Italians, from

The Coronation of Cola di Rienzo

ancient times brothers and sons of the sacred Roman people, we have made one and all the citizens of the states of sacred Italy Roman citizens, and we admit them to the election of the empire which has devolved rationally upon the sacred Roman people. And we have decreed that the election is to be conducted in the City with solemnity and maturity by the voices of twenty-four old electors. Some of these have been reserved in the City, the rest we have distributed through sacred Italy just as it is provided in the capitularies and ordinances in regard to this matter. We desire, indeed, to renew more firmly the ancient union with all the magistrates from the cities of sacred Italy and with you. And sacred Italy now for a long time prostrated, until now torn by many quarrels and degraded by those who ought to govern her in peace and justice—by those very men who have assumed the names of emperor and augustus, not fearing to come against their promise, the name not answering for the accomplishment— we desire to free from all its risk of degradation and lead it back to its former condition of ancient glory, and so to augment it that, having tasted the sweetness of peace, it may by the grace of the Holy Ghost flourish better than ever a nation has flourished in other parts of the world. For we intend, the Holy Ghost granting success, when the aforesaid limit of the Pentecost is passed, happily to promote, through the sacred Roman people and those to whom we give the votes of the imperial election, some Italian whom unity of race and suitability of nation may induce to a zeal for Italy according to the inspiration of the Holy Ghost, who has deigned piously to regard sacred Italy itself, so that we may observe the name of Augustus which the Roman people, nay with Divine inspiration, has granted and assigned, through the pleasing action of accomplished facts.

14. *Letter of Rienzo to Clement VI.* (October 11, 1347).

May Omnipotent God grant me an auditor, and may He hear my desire, that my words may not be burdensome for your holiness. My discourse is with simple heart, and my lips bespeak a pure purpose. . . .

Secondly, by the witness of God, who watches my ways and numbers all my footsteps, no greed for dignity, but the desire for the common good and safety of all the people, led me to assume this administration in which my whole body has been, and is, fevered without any rest. . . .

Thirdly, that, inasmuch as it pleases your holiness that I be dismissed from this administration through the favor of removal, considering holy and just whatever is a pleasure and a favor to your holiness, I am ready to give up the administration, disposed never to go contrary to your best wishes. And to this end it is not necessary to fatigue the curia and deafen the whole world with legal proceedings; for your one least courier would have and will suf-

The Coronation of Cola di Rienzo

fice when it shall please you; for God is greater than man, and you are greater than the kings and princes of the world. It grieves me if the opinion of my purity is beguiled; it grieves me if belial actions prevail over good works; it grieves me that out of a purity of conscience you do not think of the wiles of others nor beware of their treachery, but lean to those, some of whom are ever seeking to have a tyranny rule in the City, while the rest, moved by a hatred of the nation, wish to destroy the City utterly so that the church may never be brought back there. Since the reformation of the City demanded more elegant provision than the other cities of the world, they strive incessantly in many and various ways to assail my innocence. If I did receive the bath of knighthood in the basin in which Constantine was baptized for which I am blamed, why shall that which was allowed a pagan in cleansing himself of leprosy not be allowed to a Christian cleansing the City and the world of leprosy? And why is a stone, that stands in a temple into which it is permitted and a duty to enter, more holy than the temple which confers sanctity to the stone? Why is a man with a contrite heart, who is allowed to take the body of Christ for his salvation, not permitted to enter a stone font which, too, was held of no account through disuse? As if it seemed to those who blame this act that the entrance was made without devotion, that the font was more noble than the

very body of our Lord, Jesus Christ, which not only
I think it a sin to think and believe, but consider
the thought of an infidel! And if I am said to have
added names to myself and amplified my titles, and
to have assumed various crowns of leaves, what reference does it have to the faith to have renewed the
ancient Roman names of offices with ancient rites?

And it is not true that I was chosen [to office] with
your vicar. Nay, I stood forth chosen alone by all
the people; yea, verily, by the Holy Ghost, who had
aroused the spirit of a younger boy for the safety
of the Roman people. Your vicar, however, I
associated with myself, not of necessity, but for the
honor and reverence of your most clement holiness;
when his pusillanimity had been discovered and indulged for many days, the people unanimously reestablished me alone. Therefore, if God had permitted me to be promoted to the knighthood and
crowned with the tribunitian laurel, He knew that
it was not for the empty honor—for I know not how
long I may live, since a man's life may be ended between morning and night—that I assumed the name
of knight, but only for the office of tribune and
for the honor of the Holy Ghost by whom it pleased
Him to have my knighthood assigned. This is the
reason that my insignificant self was promoted to
that office on the feast of the Pentecost, which is
rightly the feast of the Holy Ghost; that I have and
do wish to ascribe the favor of the administration of

The Coronation of Cola di Rienzo

this office to the Holy Ghost; and that in Him, and not myself, do I glory, and in the charity of His piety am I comforted.

But the other frivolous charges which scheming tongues fix upon me to my blame, I think it more seemly to pass over, for by prudent minds these are utterly derided. I do not omit [to say], therefore, that if your consideration does and will regard the facts of the citation of the princes and the ordination in your City, you may know clearly that nothing but good and pure intention moved me; and if, in that summons, the Bavarian was called the duke of Bavaria, that did not proceed from a malicious zeal, since I do and will consider him constantly for what the holy mother church and your holiness consider him. Concerning the lord king of Bohemia, you have known if his predecessors have left such a memory of their deeds in the City and in all Italy that his advent should have been fittingly welcomed. Nay, through the coming of such an emperor the City is now bereft of many houses that were destroyed; its churches are dilapidated, and their treasures rapaciously depleted; and at Rome and in all Italy strife raged, and murders were numberless. And Italy is not from experience disposed to tolerate so harmful an entrance. . . .

Because if the meaning and effect of the deeds done is inspected, it was fitting that, in the font of the most Christian emperor Constantine, first dower

of the church, there should bathe another by whose
righteous constancy the rights of the holy Church
have been preserved; and just as Constantine was
purged of leprosy and infidelity, so this one would be
purged of the vice of tyrants; as the church was endowed by the former, so it has been freed from its
oppressors by the latter. And verily, in the land of
the saints has breathed again the church to whose
dominion I was desirous to subdue all kings and
princes; and, God granting, so it shall be. Nor did
this take place without clear miracles and omens;
and all the crowns of leaves which I received were
taken from the triumphal arch of the same Constantine, and thus it befell that his arch should
have supplied the tribunitian crown whose font had
served the knighting. . . .

Therefore legal proceedings based upon frivolous
charges could not be instituted against me, who did
and is proceeding against the rebels of the church,
the promoter of liberty, peace, and justice, without
the amazement, nay, the prostration of soul and mind
of all the people of the City, of the province of Rome,
and of all Italy. Likewise, most holy father, I
beseech that you guard against false prophets, and
that God may grant you to find out happily whether
the people of Italy or of any other nation have been
more faithful to the apostolic see. . . . May your
holiness therefore consider if it would be to the honor
of the church to have the City and the province,

The Coronation of Cola di Rienzo

which are now free, relapse into their former servitude. . . .

>Your humble creature,
>NICOLAUS, Tribune Augustus.

15. *Letter of Clement VI. to the Papal Legate* (October 12, 1347).

. . . Although an election of this kind could not at all be made without our permission, since we have complete dominion in the said city—the aforesaid people unanimously and heartily granted all the offices of the said city as pertain to them, to us, upon our promotion to the apex of apostolic dignity, and we took them under certain protestations, as you know—yet because the said bishop and Nicolaus said that they had taken this office to our honor and to that of the Roman church, and because through their administration many boons are said to have accrued to the same city, people, and surrounding land, we established them as rectors of the aforesaid city and district, to rule according to our good pleasure. We did this in the hope that they would rule the people in peace, correcting the evils and righting the wrongs, and that they would persevere peacefully in the cultivation of justice, and that, showing to us and the same church due reverence and devout obedience, they would keep its lands and rights unimpaired and protect them with their strength. And as the same Nicolaus, not content with the office of rector, but using for himself alone the title of tribune and various other titles usurped by him, has done and is doing unceasingly many things against the honor and to the prejudice of this same church; and also, as from these excesses of his he has and is rendering the said people, as much as is possible, odious to the said church and abominable to the whole world, grave trouble can threaten them in time, and other things which it shall seem to your prudence ought to be said. And let it not be kept silent how this aforesaid Nicolaus profaned by his damnable boldness the stone font in which the power of Divine Mercy through St. Sylvester regenerated Constantine, of Divine memory, with the water of the sacred baptism and miraculously cleansed him of the contagion of lepers, and which was kept in the sanctuary of the venerable church of the Lateran with veneration as a sacred object. Into this he, filthy with the contagion of his vices and forgetful of its original condition, immersed himself to receive the girdle of knighthood. And do you also see to it that he abstain from such depraved acts and profane excesses, from occupying and usurping the lands and rights against the said church, from imposing unusual burdens upon those subjects, and also from [offending] against the whole world and especially against the said vicar and our beloved sons, the nobles of the city, and against our most beloved daughter in Christ, Joanna, the illustrious queen of Sicily. . . . And in regard to the secret

The Coronation of Cola di Rienzo

treaty which he has with our most beloved son in Christ, Lewis, the illustrious king of Hungary; in regard to the citation of our most beloved son in Christ, Charles, illustrious king of the Romans, of the Electors, princes of the German Empire and of Ludwig of Bavaria, reproved by the just judgment of God, and the same Church, whom he did not with his polluted lips blush to call duke of Bavaria; in regard to the laws illegally promulgated by him; and in regard to the general revocation of previous concessions in derogation of the Primacy, as it seems, and of the power of the same church which he presumed to make in fact, though they had no substance; on condition that he solemnly, and by decree, desires to revoke [these matters], and does other things which shall seem necessary to your prudence for the correction of so great a fault and transgression; and if he is willing not to go beyond the proper bounds but, content with the rule of the same city, is willing to revoke what has been attempted by him, as has been aforesaid, to the prejudice of the said church and the world, and to pledge an oath of loyalty to us and our successors, do you suffer him to remain in the office granted to him by us, either alone or with the vicar whom he is said to have expelled, or with another for the administration of the same city. Further, on the condition, as it shall seem expedient to you, that you receive from him first [the promises] that he will treat the church with due reverence and that he will not presume at all against it, its lands, and its rights, in the presence of enough cautious bondsmen and others, and with the provision that he place himself under sufficient obligation and agree that from now on a sentence of excommunication shall be brought against him which he will incur if he attempts anything against his promises, though we think and believe very probably that his promises will have little strength. But if he seems to you at all intolerable, deprive him of the office of rector, which was granted to him by us, as well as of every title usurped by him or granted to him though only in fact by the said people, and strive to make provision for the city and people with senators or with the people or with others, just as a careful consideration of time and circumstance of the affair shall seem to you expedient. For we are granting you full power in this matter through special apostolic letters which we are sending to you along with the present letter and which you are to use as you shall recognize most effectively. None the less, if the aforesaid Nicolaus, fixed in his reprehensible idea, cannot be recalled from his rash precipitance and perchance scorns to revoke what he has attempted, to restore the lands occupied by him, and to do the other things which shall seem to your prudence that he ought to do, it seems expedient to us and our brothers that you have the apostolic processes and deeds against invaders and holders

The Coronation of Cola di Rienzo

of the lands of the Church made public, and though you cite him personally, do not defer to commence your proceedings against him. But since the same Nicolaus is said to have committed and done many things beyond what has been mentioned above, for which he can be regarded with the suspicion of heresy, see whether you find in him cause for a charge of heresy or of aid to heretics, and in that case do not fail to proceed against him as a heretic. . . . Finally, the letters of the Jubilee for the fiftieth year we think should be held back for the present rather than issued, since we do not know whether the aforesaid people will withdraw from that untractable man or whether they will follow him in his errors. But if, leaving him in his errors, they are disposed toward and return to the devotion and obedience of ourselves and that church, as they are bound, we shall quickly despatch letters of that import and follow them freely with pleasing favors and paternal affection in these and other matters.

Dated at Avignon, on the fourth day before the Ides of October in the sixth year of our pontificate.

16. *Letter of Pope Clement to the People of Rome* (December 3, 1347).

. . . Just as is commonly known, and as is generally and publicly declared, the aforementioned Nicolaus, not content with the office committed to himself and the aforementioned bishop, but with a different mind, impudently assumed various titles. Placing your interests last, and neglecting the common welfare which this deceitful man pretended to cherish, he covetously drove the bishop from the office in which so much greater glory had accrued to him as colleague. The bishop, cursing the damnable crimes of this Nicolaus, refused to remain in the same city. The other, fearing not the spiritual punishments and sentences to which invaders and transgressors of the land and rights of the church are liable, nor fearing the wrath of God against him, did not fear to provoke us seriously and extend his sacrilegious hands upon the lands and rights of the Church itself, and to place heavy and unusual taxes upon the inhabitants. . . . Wherefore we warn, demand, and urge you all considerately; we exhort you with wholesome and paternal counsel to meditate carefully over the things that have been done and the many others which can occur to your prudent consideration. Desist from all support, counsel, aid, and favor of this Nicolaus, and leave to his errors him whose iniquity crawls like a serpent, spreads like an ulcer, and infects like poison. Shun him as a sick beast that contaminates the whole herd with its disease. Persist in reverence and obedience to the church, receive its admonitions humbly in your wonted manner, and fulfil them effectively. For if, as we hope and believe, you persist in obedience

and affection with paternal and sincere devotion
to us and the aforesaid church, we will reward you
as spiritual, devoted, and loyal sons of the church,
with grateful favors and pleasing thanks before the
Lord.

APPENDIX

A Specimen Report Based on the Narratives in Problem III

To illustrate better the method of working out the exercises, question number 3, Problem III, page 101, has been outlined and then put in the form that a final report might have.

1. Outline

What changes were made in the plan of attack during the siege? What reasons can be found for such changes?
I. Original location of the different leaders.
   1. On the north.
      (a) Robert of Normandy (*Anonymous*, p. 103, ll. 7–11; *Raymond*, p. 115, ll. 18–22).
      (b) Robert of Flanders (*Raymond*, p. 115, ll. 17, 18; *Anonymous*, p. 103, ll. 11–13).
      Godfrey (*Raymond*, p. 115, ll. 17, 18).
   2. On the west.
      (a) Godfrey (*Anonymous*, p. 103, ll. 13, 14).
      Tancred (*Anonymous*, p. 103, l. 14).
      (b) Raymond (*Raymond*, p. 115, ll. 22–25).
II. Change of position on the north.
   1. Reasons for the change (*Anonymous*, p. 106, ll. 22; p. 107, l. 5; *Raymond*, p. 127, ll. 5–12; p. 127, l. 27; p. 128, l. 5).

Appendix

  2. How the change was made (*Anonymous*, p. 107, ll. 1–5; *Raymond*, p. 127, ll. 12–27; *Fulk*, p. 111, l. 15; p. 112, l. 5).
  3. Final location (*Anonymous*, p. 107, ll. 4, 5; *Raymond*, p. 127, ll. 17–19).
III. Raymond's move to Mt. Zion on the south.
  1. Reasons for this change.
     (a) The real reason (*Raymond*, p. 115, ll. 25–30).
     (b) The reason assigned (*Raymond*, p. 116, ll. 4–15).
  2. Evidence of Raymond's location on Mt. Zion (*Anonymous*, p. 103, ll. 15, 16; p. 107, ll. 7–9; p. 108, l. 6; *Fulk*, p. 112, ll. 14–16).
  3. Where Raymond made his final attack (*Raymond*, p. 132, ll. 7–11; p. 133, ll. 2–5; *Anonymous*, p. 108, ll. 12–21; *Fulk*, p. 113, ll. 19, 20).

2. Discussion

Apparently the crusaders were not numerous enough to besiege the city on all sides, so they selected what seemed to be the most vulnerable places in the fortifications. Thus the city was attacked on two sides; on the south by Raymond of Toulouse, and on the north by the other leaders.

Robert of Normandy first stationed himself near the old church of St. Stephen (*Anonymous*, p. 103, ll. 7–11; *Raymond*, p. 115, ll. 18–22). To the west of this position was Robert of Flanders. According to Raymond's account (p. 115, ll. 17, 18), Godfrey was also on the north, but this may refer to the change of position that was made just before the final attack. The *Anonymous* states (p. 103, ll. 13, 14) that Godfrey and Tancred first located their camp on the west, probably well to the northwest.

Parallel Source Problems in Medieval History

The original position of these men and their followers probably extended from the center of the northern side of the city around the corner to the west. Raymond says (p. 115, ll. 22-25) that the count of Toulouse first pitched his camp on the west, probably just south of Godfrey and Tancred, but the other writers make no mention of this.

All three writers agree that this first position on the northwest was changed (*Anonymous*, p. 107, ll. 1-5; *Raymond*, p. 127, ll. 12-19; *Fulk*, p. 111, l. 15; p. 112, l. 5). The Saracens had so greatly strengthened the wall at this point, while the crusaders were constructing their machines, that the leaders decided that it would be better to attack in another place, where the defenders were not so well prepared for the defense. Raymond (p. 127, l. 17; p. 128, l. 5) further says that the ground was more level at the place which was selected for the final attack. That this was an important consideration is shown by the difficulties that Raymond had in moving his machines up close to the wall (*Anonymous*, p. 108, ll. 6-12).

The machinery, which had been constructed near the location of the first camp, was moved during the night. This was a difficult piece of work, and in the morning the Saracens were greatly surprised to note that the crusaders were prepared to attack the wall in a new quarter and that they had moved their camp (*Raymond*, p. 127, ll. 22-27) as well as their machines.

The new location was almost a mile from the first position of the army. Raymond says that the northern part of the army was located in the space between the church of St. Stephen and the valley of Jehosaphat, which is on the eastern side of the city. The *Anonymous* states (p. 107, ll. 1-5) that the machines and the tower were dragged

Appendix

to the eastern side, but he may mean that they were moved to the east of the first camp. Our other writer, *Fulk* (p. 111, l. 19; p. 112, l. 1), says that the tower was moved by night and set up at a corner of the city. It would thus seem that the final attack of this wing of the army was made on the northeast corner.

Raymond (p. 115, ll. 22-30) says that the count of Toulouse, who had first established his camp on the western side of the city, while reconnoitering, decided that Mt. Zion was a better position. He decided to move his camp, but encountered opposition on the part of the other leaders. He made the change, but according to his chaplain became very unpopular because of his action.[1] (*Raymond*, p. 116, ll. 13-23).

It would seem that the real reason for this change was the irregular character of the land to the west, for a ravine would have made it difficult to move the siege engines close to the walls. However, this was not the reason that the count gave. According to the story of his chaplain, he was so much impressed by the church on Mt. Zion and its sacred associations that he became much alarmed lest the Saracens should get possession of it and defile it. He thus tried to make out that he was really doing a pious act in occupying such a holy spot. (See the speech that *Raymond* puts into the mouth of the count, p. 116, ll. 4-13.) Raymond already had the reputation of being more or less of a hypocrite, for he had used the holy lance that was found at Antioch to further his own interests. Here again he was trying to allay the jealousies of the other leaders by trying to convince them that he was

---

[1] This is an evidence of the fear that the other leaders had of Raymond's ambition.

guided solely by religious motives. It would seem that the other crusaders knew his methods, for eventually he was not able to persuade his men to follow him to the new location that he had selected for his camp, except by bribing them with money.

Although *Raymond* is the only writer who says that the count of Toulouse first located his camp to the west of the city, there is little reason to doubt that his final position was on Mt. Zion (*Anonymous*, p. 103, ll. 15, 16; p. 107, ll. 7–9; p. 108, l. 6; *Fulk*, p. 112, ll. 14–16). Just what part of the wall he attacked is more difficult to determine.

It would seem likely that Raymond attacked the western part of the southern wall, or the southwest corner. However, we are told that the tower of David was surrendered to him and that "that gate at which the pilgrims had always been accustomed to pay tribute" was opened (*Anonymous*, p. 108, ll. 19–21). The gate by the tower of David, the David or Joppa gate, which opened on the Joppa road, from which port the pilgrims usually came. Why Raymond entered by this gate may be explained by his failure to force an entrance through the wall before the other division of the crusading army had done so at the northwest corner. Moreover, as the gate was opened from within, Raymond and his men undoubtedly gave up their efforts to force their way in at the place where they had been working, and sought an easier entrance through the western gate.

INDEX

ADELAIDE, Marchioness, 66, 89.
Adhemar, bishop of Puy, 123, 133.
Agnes, empress, mother of Henry IV. of Germany, 30, 74.
Alan of Beccles, 147.
Albara, bishop of, 126.
Albert of Stade, 142.
Albornoz, cardinal, 183.
Alcuin, 10.
Amadeus, 45.
Angelo Malabreme, 219.
Angers, 148, 150, 151, 164.
Annals of Augsburg, 33–34; quoted, 40–41.
Annales of Dunstable, 142; quoted, 150.
Annales Laurissenses, 9; quoted, 13–16.
Annales Laurishamenses, 9; quoted, 16–18.
Annales Stadenses, 142; quoted, 150.
Anonymi Vita Heinrici IV. Imperatoris, 37; quoted, 81–84.
Anselm, bishop of Lucca, 73.
Antioch, 96–97, 100–101.
Archardus of Montemerlus, 105, 120.
Arno, Archbishop, 20.
Arnulf, 36.
Arnulfi Gesta, 36; quoted, 74–75.
Augsburg, 72–73, 77, 84.
Augsburg, bishop of, 70.

Avignon, 177–178, 180, 182, 183.
Azzo, Margrave, 48, 52.

BABENBERG, bishop of, 51.
Baldwin, Duke, 96, 100.
Basel, 57, 69.
Beneventians, Pepin's expedition against, 13.
Bernhard, Bishop, 20.
Bernoldi Chronicon, 36; quoted, 72–74.
Bertha, empress, wife of Henry IV. of Germany, 30.
Berthold of Reichenau, 35.
Bertholdi Annales, 35; quoted, 56–71.
Besançon, 44, 64.
Bethlehem, 122.
Blanche, queen of France, 159, 161–162.
Bohemond, 96, 100.
Bonitho, bishop of Sutri, 37.
Bremen, bishop of, 69, 91.
Bruno, 36–37.
Brunonis de Bello Saxonico, 36; quoted, 75–81.
Bryce's *Holy Roman Empire*, 12.
Burgundy, 44.
Byzantine empire, 6, 95.

CAMPULUS, 22–23.
Canossa, 33–34, 36–38, 40, 65, 72, 75, 84, 86, 89, 91.
Carolingians, recognized defend-

Parallel Source Problems in Medieval History

ers of Christianity, 6; historians of, 8–12.
Chalons, archdeacon of, 159, 161, 163.
Charles of Bohemia, German emperor, 179, 182–183, 200, 206, 214, 224, 233.
Charles the Fat, 11.
Charles the Great, crowned, 6; 15, 17–19, 21; protects Leo III., 7, 14, 20; chronicles relating to, 9–12; journey to Rome, 13, 16, 18, 24; reply to Byzantine emperor, 25, 26.
Chronica of Alberic of Tres Fontes, 142; quoted, 149.
Chronica Majora, 141.
Chronicon Anglicanum, 142; quoted, 150.
Chronicon Fiscamense, 142; quoted, 151.
Chronographia of Theophanis, 10; quotation from, 18–19.
Cinis (Mt. Cenis), 45.
Citation of the German Emperor and Electors, 185; quoted, 203–206.
Clement VI., 180, 183; letters to Cola di Rienzo, 190–192, 216; summoned by Rienzo to return to Rome, 200; letters from Rienzo to, 207–211, 217–220, 226–230; letters to papal legate, 216, 231–235; writes people of Rome, 235–237.
Cluny, abbot of, 66, 86, 89, 91.
Cluny, monastery of, 29.
Cola di Rienzo, career of, 177; early history of, 179; goes to Avignon, 180; made tribune, 181; excommunication and flight of, 182; imprisonment and death, 183, 203; titles used by, 189; writes letters to Florence, 192, 222–225; writes to a friend at Avignon, 193–195; receives knighthood, 196–202; citation to Emperor and Electors, 203–206; writes Clement VI., 207–211, 217–219, 226–230; summary by Giovanni Villani of his acts, 212–214; coronation of, 214–215; writes to Raynold Orsini, 220–222.

College of Cardinals, 31.
Cologne, archbishop of, 30, 206.
Colonna family, 178, 196, 212.
Como, bishop of, 71.
Conrad, emperor of Germany, 30.
Constance, 36, 57.
Constantin Kopronymos, 10.
Constantinople, 4–5, 100.
Conventus Oppenheimensis, 34; quoted, 41–42.
Cosheim, Oudalric, bishop of, 51.
Crusades, 95–98.
Cunibert, Bishop, 20.

De Gestis Karoli Magni, 11; quotation from, 23.
De Monarchia of Dante, 179.
Donizo, 37–38.
Donizonis Vita Matildis, 37; quoted, 85–87.

EASTER, computation of dates for, 8.
Edessa, 96, 100.
Einhard, 9–10, 18.
English "nation," 139.
Erlung, bishop of Würzburg, 37.
Eustace, Count, 107.

FÉCAMP, 142.
Flaccus, 20.
Florence, 184–186, 192–193, 211–213, 222–225.
Foresheim, 32, 35, 41, 60, 73, 79.
Frangipani family, 178.

Index

Frankish kings, 4, 6, 8.
Frederic II., German emperor, 143.
French "nation," 139.
Fulda, monastery of, 10.
Fulk of Chartres, 100, 109.

GÆTANI FAMILY, 178.
Galdemarus, Count, 120.
Gartanus, count of Fondi, 219.
Gaston of Beert, 109, 125–126.
Geneva, 64.
George Synkellos, 10.
Gerald, bishop of Osria, 73.
Germar, 20.
Gesta Francorum et aliorum Hierosolymitanorum, 99; quoted, 103–109.
Gesta Francorum Jerusalem expugnantium, 100; quoted, 109–115.
Gesta Ludovici, 141; quoted, 148–149.
Giovanni Villani: Historia Universalis, 185; quoted, 211–214.
Godfrey, duke of Bouillon, 96, 103, 106–107, 112, 115, 132.
Greeks, 97.
Gregory VII. (Hildebrand), 29; threatens Henry IV. with excommunication, 31; forced from Rome by Henry, 32; excommunicates Henry, 32; receives Henry at Canossa, 40–42, 48, 50, 53, 67, 74, 78, 84, 86; charges against Henry made to, 81–82.
Gregory IX., 143; letter to bishop of Paris, 158–160; letter to bishops of Le Mans and Senlis and the archdeacon of Chalons, 161–162; letter to King Louis and Queen Blanche, 162–163; letter to the Masters and Students at Paris and Angers, 164–165; letter to the Masters and Students of Paris, 165–171; letter to Odo, abbot of Saint Germain-des-Près, 172; letter to King Louis, 173–174.
Guelf and Ghibelline, 219.

HADRIAN I., pope, 6, 19.
Helingot, 20.
Henry III., German emperor, appoints popes, 29; death of, 30.
Henry III., king of England, letter to Masters and Students of Paris, 152.
Henry IV., German emperor, 29; minority and marriage, 30; subdues the Saxons, 31; excommunicated by pope, 31, 82; signs agreement at Oppenheim, 34, 40–42, 57–58, 72; war with Rudolph, 41; at Canossa, 43–50, 53, 67, 73, 75, 78, 84; oath of, 90–91.
Henry VII., German emperor, 177, 179.
Hersfeld, monastery of, 34.
Hildebald, Archbishop, 20.
Hildebrand (*see* GREGORY VII.).
Historia Francorum qui Ceperunt Jerusalem, 100; quoted, 115–133.
Holy Land, 95, 98.

INNOCENT III., 140, 143.
Innocent VI., 183.
Irene, Empress, 6.

JERUSALEM, arrival of crusaders before, 96, 103; siege and capture of, 106–113, 117–118, 126–133; description of city by Fulk of Chartres, 110.
Jesse, Bishop, 20.
Joanna, queen of Naples, 178, 182, 232.
John Blund, 147.
John Colonna, 220.

John of Columna, 142.
John of Vico, 181, 194.
Joppa, 105, 120–121, 128.
Jordan, river, 122.
Justinian, Emperor, 4.

LAMBERT, of Hersfeld, 33, 34.
Lamberti Annales, 34–35; quoted, 42–56.
Lausanne, bishop of, 69.
Le Mans, bishop of, 159, 161, 163.
Leo III., protected by Charles the Great, 7, 19; *Life of*, 11; receives Charles in Rome, 13; purges himself of charges, 14, 21, 24; crowns Charles, 15, 17–19, 21.
Lethold, 107.
Letters of Clement VI. to the Papal Legate, 186; quoted, 216, 231–236.
Letter of Clement to the People of Rome, 187; quoted, 235–237.
Letter of Clement VI. to Raymond, Bishop of Orvieto, 184; quoted, 190–192.
Letter of Gregory to the German princes, 38; quoted, 87–90.
Letter of Rienzo to the City of Florence, 186; quoted, 222–225.
Letters of Rienzo to Clement VI., 185, 186; quoted, 207–211, 217–219, 226–230.
Letter of Rienzo to the Commune of Florence, 184; quoted, 192–193.
Letter of Rienzo to a Friend at Avignon, 184; quoted, 193–195.
Letter of Rienzo to Rinaldo Orsini at Avignon, 186; quoted, 220–222.
Lewis, king of Hungary, 233.
Lex Regia, Tablet of, 180.

Liber Bonithonis ad Amicum, 37; quoted, 84–85.
Liber Caroli, 6.
Liber Pontificalis, 11, 19.
Lombards, encroachments of, 6.
Lorsch, abbey of, 9.
Louis IX., king of France, 153, 159, 161–162, 171, 173.
Ludwig of Bavaria, 177–179, 200, 206, 214, 224, 233.
Luttich, bishop of, 57.

MAGDEBURG, 36, 56.
Mainz, 13, 16, 41; archbishop of, 57, 206.
Mare Historiarum, 142; quoted, 151.
Marsiglio of Padua, 179.
Mathew of Paris, 141; quoted, 145–148.
Matilda, countess of Tuscany, 37–38; urges Gregory VII. to retire to Canossa, 48, 74, 84; intervention of, 66, 86, 89; death of mother, 85.
Michael, Byzantine emperor, 24.
Milan, archbishopric of, 31, 36.
Münster, bishop of, 57.

NAUMBURG, bishop of, 68–69.
Nicholas of Farnham, 147.
Nomentum, 13.
Norman "nation," 139, 147.
Notker Balbus, 11.
Notre Dame, school of, 137.

ODO, abbot of Saint Germain-des-Près, 172.
Opertus, Margrave, 63.
Oppenheim, 32; Henry's agreement at, 34, 40, 57, 72.
Order of the Provisors, Closing the University of Paris, 151.
Orleans, 151.
Orsini family, 178, 195–196, 212.
Otto, Bishop, 20.
Otto, duke of Bavaria, 30, 80.

Index

PADERBORN, 7.
Papacy, 5–6; crusade against marriage of clergy, and simony, 29; frees itself from imperial control, 31.
Parens Scientiarum, 165.
Paris, bishop of, 146; letter from Gregory IX. to, 158–160.
Paris, educational center, 137, 139 (*see* UNIVERSITY OF PARIS).
Pascal, 22–23.
Patavia, bishop of, 57, 61, 76.
Patriarch of Jerusalem, 14.
Pavia, 41, 71.
Pepin, 6, 13.
Perugia, 211, 213.
Peter Desiderius, 123, 130.
Petrarch, 179.
Philip III., king of France, 141.
Philip Augustus, 139, 143, 153.
Picard "nation," 139, 146–147.
Priscian, 170.
Program of the Coronation of Cola di Rienzo, 186; quoted, 214–215.

QUINTIUS, 71.

RALPH COGGESHALL, 142, 150.
Ralph of Maidenstone, 147.
Ramla, 120–121.
Ravenna, 13, 18.
Raymond of Agiles, 100, 115.
Raymond of Orvieto, 181, 190.
Raymond Piletus, 104–105; takes part in siege of Jerusalem, 106, 108, 112–113, 115; moves camp to Mount Zion, 116; goes toward Joppa, 120; fights at Ramla, 121.
Raymond of Taurina, 104.
Raymond, count of Toulouse, 96, 100.
Regina, 87.
Rheims, 151.
Robert, count of Flanders, 103, 112, 115, 125, 127.

Robert, king of Naples, 178.
Robert of Normandy, 100, 103, 112, 125, 127.
Romain of St. Angelo, papal legate, 147.
Roman Empire, disappearance of, 3; likeness of Charles the Great's empire to, 4, 8; relation to Church, 5.
Rome, barbarians' respect for, 4–5; Charles the Great's journey to, 7, 13, 17; Cola di Rienzo ruler of, 177, 181; rivalry of great families in, 178.
Rottegar, 20.
Rudolph, German emperor, 32, 35, 37, 41, 73, 80–81.

ST. ÆGIDIUS, count of, 103–104; takes part in siege of Jerusalem, 107.
St. Blaise, monastery of, 36.
St. Gall, Monk of, 11.
St. Genevieve, school of, 137.
St. Marcel, quarrel at, 145–146.
St. Stephen, church of, in Jerusalem, 103.
St. Victor's, school of, 137.
Salic kings, 31.
Samothrace, 10.
Sardica, Council of, 56.
Saxons, 30, 32, 36, 43, 75, 79–80, 81.
Senlis, bishop of, 159, 161, 163.
Siegfrid, archbishop of Mainz, 8.
Sienna, 211.
Spires, 57, 60.
Spring of Siloam, 105, 109, 118.
Stephen, count of Blois, 100.
Strasburg, bishop of, 57, 69.
Suetonius, 10.
Swabians, 79–81.

TANCRED, 100; prepares to attack Jerusalem, 103; protects

prisoners, 109; steals and restores gold from Sepulcher, 114; occupies Bethlehem, 122; enters Jerusalem, 132.
Temple of Solomon, 108, 113, 132.
Theophanis, 10–11.
Titles Used by Cola di Rienzo, 184, 189–190.
Todi, 211.
Toul, bishop of, 60.
Treves, bishop of, 57, 59, 61; archbishop of, 206.
Tribur, 32.
Turin, 64.
Turks, 95, 97, 105, 120, 125.

ULM, 57.
University of Paris, masters' power in, 139–140; dispersion, 147, 150–151, 161, 163; return to Paris, 148, 150; privilege issued by kings to, 153–158; regulation of affairs by Gregory IX., 166–171.
Utrecht, 57.

VERCELLI, bishop of, 52, 68, 84, 91.
Verdun, bishop of, 57.
Vico Scotto, 199.
Vita Anonymi di Cola di Rienzo, 184; quoted, 196–203.
Vita Karoli, 9–10; quotation from, 18–19.
Vita Leonis III., 11; quotation from, 19–22.

WERNER, bishop of Merseburg, 36.
William of Auxerre, 165.
William of Durham, 147.
William Ebriacus, 128.
William of Nangis, 141, 148.
William Richau, 126.
William of Sabram, 105, 120.
William Ugo, 123.
Worms, 32, 42, 58; bishop of, 76.

YSOARDUS, Count, 123.

ZACHARY, 14.
Zeitz, bishop of, 52, 55.

THE END

www.ingramcontent.com/pod-product-compliance
Lightning Source LLC
Chambersburg PA
CBHW062011220426
43662CB00010B/1284